THE NEED AND THE BLESSING OF PRAYER

The Need
and the Blessing
of Prayer

A new translation of
Father Rahner's book on prayer

Karl Rahner, S.J.

Translated by
Bruce W. Gillette

Introduction by
Harvey D. Egan, S.J.

A Liturgical Press Book

THE LITURGICAL PRESS
Collegeville, Minnesota

Cover design by Ann Blattner

Originally published in German as *Von der Not und dem Segen des Gebetes*. © by Verlag Herder GmbH & Co. KG.

2	3	4	5	6	7	8

Library of Congress Cataloging-in-Publication Data

Rahner, Karl, 1904–
    [Von der Not und dem Segen des Gebetes. English]
    The need and the blessing of prayer / Karl Rahner ; translated by Bruce W. Gillette ; introduction by Harvey D. Egan.
       p.   cm.
    "A revised edition of On prayer."
    Includes bibliographical references.
    ISBN 0-8146-2453-7
    1. Prayer—Christianity. I. Rahner, Karl, 1904– On prayer.
II. Title.
BV210.2.R2613   1997
248.3'2—dc21   97–7368
                                                          CIP

Contents

Introduction

"Strengthened by the Church's sacrament and accompanied by the prayers of his Jesuit brothers, shortly after completing his eightieth year, Father Karl Rahner has gone home to God. . . . He had loved the Church and his religious Order and spent himself in their service." So read part of the official Jesuit announcement of the death of Father Karl Rahner, S.J., on March 30, 1984. And with his death, the Church lost one of her most loyal sons.

Rahner has been called one of the greatest theologians of this century, *the* voice of the Second Vatican Council, "the quiet mover of the Roman Catholic Church," and the "father of the Catholic Church in the twentieth century." However, he preferred to refer to himself as someone who was "not particularly industrious," who "went to bed early," and who was a "poor sinner." In fact, "all I want to be," he emphasized, "even in this work [of theology], is a human being, a Christian, and, as well as I can, a priest of the Church."[1]

I first met Father Rahner in 1969 when he graciously accepted the invitation to celebrate my first Mass with me and to spend the day with my family and friends. During my four years of doctoral studies under his direction, from 1969 to 1973, I found him to be at once utterly brilliant, shockingly creative, traditional in the best sense, original, provocative, balanced, and healing. A passion for hard work, detail, precision, and an

---

1. W. Ernst Böhm, ed., "Selbstporträt," *Forscher und Gelehrte* (Stuttgart: Battenberg, 1966) 21. For further autobiographical information, see *Karl Rahner—I Remember: An Autobiographical Interview with Meinold Krauss*, trans. and intro. Harvey D. Egan (New York: Crossroad, 1985).

impatience with mental laziness, "whoring after relevance," and bureaucratic incompetence stamped his personality.

And who would not be fascinated by a theologian who loved carnivals, ice cream, large shopping malls, and being driven at very high speeds—one whose olfactory curiosity cost him many dollars in New York when a large department store demanded that he purchase all the perfume bottles he had opened? However, most impressive of all were the simplicity, holiness, and priestliness of his Jesuit and theological life.

At this theologian's crypt I often prayed. I still pray *to* him. It astonishes me how often he appears in my dream life. I've said and written that he is the father of my theological life and of my heart.

When only twenty years old Rahner published his first article, "Why We Need to Pray."[2] For all practical purposes his first book was a book of prayers, *Encounters with Silence*;[3] his last book, *Prayers for a Lifetime*.[4] In fact, explicit prayer and penetrating reflection on prayer punctuated his entire theological life. Even many essays in his meaty *Theological Investigations* often end by shading into prayer. Thus Rahner stands in a long line of great Christian theologians who were likewise great teachers of prayer.

Much of Rahner's theology flows out of and then leads back into encounters with the saving, silent presence of the mystery of God's love for us in the crucified and risen Christ—and does so without dissolving theology's necessarily critical and rational

2. "Warum uns das Beten not tut," *Leuchtturm* 18 (1924–5) 10–1.

3. James M. Demske, trans. (Westminster, Md.: Newman Press, 1960). One commentator (Robert Kress, *A Rahner Handbook* [Atlanta: John Knox Press, 1982] 94) describes the "mood" of the prayers in *Encounters* and this newly translated volume "a bit heavy—even lugubrious—for today's readers. Written shortly after World War II, they intensely reflect the mood of misery of those years." I do not share that view. I personally know several people from many walks of life whose lives were profoundly changed by reading Rahner's books on and of prayer. One example—a friend who worked in a halfway house for troubled teenagers found her copy of *Encounters* in the hands of a young woman who exclaimed: "Who is this person? He prays just like me!"

4. Albert Raffelt, ed., translator's name not given (New York: Crossroad, 1984).

function. To some extent one can view Rahner's theology as prayer seeking understanding, as kneeling with the mind before holy mystery with Christ in the Spirit.

Rahner views the human person as essentially one called to pray. He also highlights prayer as the fundamental act of human existence, the act which embraces the entire person—the great religious act. For Rahner, to pray is to be. He sees Christ's humanity as prayer's perfect paradigm: total, unconditional surrender to holy mystery. Likewise, he considers the God-question and the prayer-question as two sides of the same coin.

Prayer, to Rahner, is the last moment of speech before the silence; the act of self-surrender just before the incomprehensible God disposes of one; the reflection immediately preceding the act of letting oneself fall—after the last of one's own efforts—and full of trust—into the infinite fullness and silence that reflection can never grasp.

Rahner was never one to wear his heart on his sleeve. But he did not hesitate to pray publicly. In fact, he often prayed the Rosary while his lectures were being read to American audiences by an interpreter. He enjoyed relating how he and Cardinal Ottaviani—the same cardinal responsible for a Vatican slap on Rahner's wrist—once prayed the Rosary and the Litany of Loreto while traveling together. That the senile St. Albert the Great could do nothing more at the end of his life than pray the Hail Mary impressed Rahner as a great blessing. He hailed the Jesuit custom of assigning old Jesuits the task of praying for the Society of Jesus, the "work" found after their names in the Jesuit catalogue.[5]

He once confessed that "I am also someone who has been tempted by atheism."[6] But he said in the same breath: "There is nothing more self-evident to me than God's existence."[7] When challenged by an interviewer because of his great faith despite the horrors of Nazism, Rahner said: "I believe because I pray."[8]

5. Cf. *Karl Rahner—I Remember*, esp. 64, 103. Also see Hubert Biallowons, Harvey Egan, and Paul Imhof, eds., *Karl Rahner in Dialogue: Conversations and Interviews, 1965–82* (New York: Crossroad, 1986) 242.

6. Biallowons, Egan, and Imhof, *Karl Rahner in Dialogue*, 211.

7. Ibid.

8. Ibid, 212.

Rahner—whose name is often associated with highly specula-
tive theology—never hesitated to exhort people to "pray in the
everyday."[9] By that he meant "regular prayer which is practiced
without regard to the desire and mood of the moment. . . .
Prayer at the ringing of the Angelus, the rosary by oneself or
with one's family, the silent private visit to a church and the
tabernacle outside of the times of common divine service, and
other devout practices of old customs as, for example, showing
respect while passing a church or an image of the cross, making
the sign of the cross while slicing a loaf of bread, the sign of the
cross which a child requests and receives from its parents in the
evening. . . ."[10] "Beware the person of no devotions and the
person who doesn't pray," he once said to me. For these, and for
many other reasons, I have called Rahner the church doctor of
prayer for the twentieth century.

The God who communicates his very own self to us, not an
abstract God, stands at the center of Rahner's theology of
prayer—in fact, his entire theology. Whether we are explicitly, directly conscious of it, whether we open ourselves to it, our whole
being is directed toward a holy, loving mystery who is the basis
of our entire existence. Life's secret ingredient is the grasp of
God's silent incomprehensibility before which we can only fall
dumb in adoration, before which and toward which we exist,
whether we wish to or not.[11]

The God of holy mystery, revelation, and love offers self to
everyone with a certain immediacy to share his own divine life.
For Rahner, therefore, there is no such thing as the "natural"
person because all creation is graced with the offer of God's self-
communication, even prior to any human response. This means
that there was never a time or a place in which God did not offer
himself to all persons. Hence, everyone must say freely yes or no
to God's self-offer with one's entire being. Thus, in every single
human heart, a divine-human drama is taking place—the drama

9. This volume, "Prayer in the Everyday," p. 37.
10. Ibid., p. 38.
11. This is a constant theme throughout Rahner's writings. For example, see "Man in the Presence of Absolute Mystery," *Foundations of
Christian Faith*, trans. William V. Dych (New York: Seabury, 1978) 44–89.

of God offering his very own life, which must be freely accepted or rejected by every single person.

To Rahner, God's self-offer as holy mystery, revelation, and love actually constitutes human identity. To be human in its most radical sense means to be the addressee of God's offer of self. Thus, the human person *is* an immense longing, a living pray-er, quenched only when he or she has surrendered fully to silent mystery's all-embracing spirit of love.

Rahner maintains that our deepest, primordial experience— what haunts the center of our hearts—is of a God who remains holy mystery, the word that illuminates our spirits, and the love that embraces us. This is not a particular, or "categorical," experience to which we can point. Rather, it is an experience beyond all particulars, a "transcendental" experience. It is the atmosphere in which we live, our basal spiritual metabolism, "more intimate to us than we are to ourselves," as the mystics were fond of saying. Just as we take our breathing, our beating hearts, or our own self-awareness for granted, so too may the ever-present experience of God remain overlooked, repressed, or even denied. When it comes to the experience of God in our daily lives, we are like sponges in water. We take the water for granted.

One finds this primordial experience, at least implicitly, in all personal experiences. And, to Rahner, all human experiences tend toward "an intensification which is directed towards something which one could in fact call mystical experience."[12] The immense longing contains within itself the seeds of infused contemplation, that is, mystical prayer in the strict sense, or what I prefer to call "awakened contemplation."

In God's self-communication, we actually experience God-above-us (holy mystery), God-with-us (enfleshed Word), and God-in-us (Holy Spirit). The call of holy mystery explains why we are never satisfied totally with anything in this life. The attraction of the historical crucified and risen Word explains why we are always looking for that one person who will fulfill us perfectly—whom Rahner calls the "absolute savior." The attraction

---

12. "Gradual Ascent to Christian Perfection," *Theological Investigations III*, trans. Karl-H. Kruger and Boniface Kruger (Baltimore: Helicon, 1967) 23.

of the Holy Spirit explains why our immense longing often draws us into the deepest levels of self. We are essentially ecstatic beings drawn to God's holy mystery, worldly and historical beings attracted to an absolute savior, and enstatic beings drawn to our deepest interior by the fontal fullness of the Spirit of love. In short, we are called to live and to be trinitarian prayer.

To Rahner, because *every* person experiences God at least in a hidden way and weaves the fabric of a divine life out of his or her humdrum days, Rahner speaks often of the prayer of everyday life.[13] Paradoxically, this prayer normally appears in the grayness and banality of everyday life, in contrast to the psychologically dramatic way the prayer of the great saints is manifested. The prayer of everyday things also encompasses even the most humble aspects of daily life. For example, in Rahner's meditation on sleep[14] he calls attention to the human person as free but who loses control and surrenders to the unconscious self. This self-surrender is, of course, at the heart of Rahner's prayer of daily life. The simple act of sleeping for him can be an implicit confidence in the inherent rightness, security, and goodness of the world. When questioned in his advanced years for his advice to old people, Rahner said quite simply: Live as well as you can, make new friends, socialize, take up a hobby. Yet, if one is reduced to total incapacity, that is all right because one will be more likely to place oneself in God's hands rather than in one's own. That is the prayer of daily life.

Perhaps the most easily recognized form of the prayer of everyday life is the universal experience of the immense longing. *All* persons experience the profound difference between what they want from life and what life actually gives them. Even those who have intelligence, prestige, power, wealth, reputation, health, and a loving family—those who seem to have it all—experience a profound emptiness at times.

The hunger of the heart is revealed in the mistaken belief that the thing or person that will fulfill us totally is just around the corner. We are always on the lookout for this thing or person we

13. See "Prayer in the Everyday," p. 37ff.
14. See "On Sleep," *Belief Today*, trans. M. H. Heelan (New York: Sheed & Ward, 1967) 35–6.

believe will quench our immense longing. As a child, we want the one toy; as a young person, to belong to the right group, get into the right school, or date the right person; as an adult, to obtain the right position, find the right mate, and the like. Yet when we obtain our heart's alleged desire, we soon discover it is not enough.

The heart is a lonely hunter because it is restless until it rests in God. The immense longing we feel in daily life underscores that nothing finite ultimately satisfies us, that we will settle for nothing less than perfect life and total fulfillment. In fact, the Scriptures tell us that the first temptation was to be like God, indicating that we want it all.

Because God has communicated himself to the very roots of our being, we experience God at least in a silent, hidden, and even repressed way. This ever-present experience of God, the anonymous presence of our heart's desire, is the ambience or horizon against which we experience all else. This God-experience is the cause of our dissatisfaction with life, for nothing measures up to the God who offers himself at our deepest center. The immense longing speaks to us, even if at times only in a whisper: this or that finite thing is not ultimately where we have already set our hearts. Is this not prayer, an encounter with silence?

To Rahner, the prayer of everyday life exists not only as the immense longing, or even only as the undertow, vector, or implicit call to holiness found in every person's deepest interior. It becomes more explicit in the many good and lovely experiences that punctuate even the most banal lives. Hence Rahner calls attention to joyful experiences, to the good and beautiful things of life, because they "promise and point to eternal light and everlasting life."[15] Since God can be found in all things, there is certainly an Easter faith that loves the earth, a radical prayer of joy in the world.[16]

In the Gospels one finds Jesus at wedding feasts, at banquets, changing water into wine, making food available to the hungry—

15. "Experiencing the Spirit," *The Practice of Faith: A Handbook of Contemporary Spirituality*, ed. Karl Lehmann and Albert Raffelt (New York: Crossroad, 1983) 81.

16. "The Ignatian Mysticism of Joy in the World," 277–93.

in short, eating and drinking in a way that shocked the Pharisees. Jesus marveled at the birds of the air, the flowers of the field, and rejoiced in the many joys found in ordinary life. Is this not the prayer of daily life?

As Rahner says, "The good things in life are not only for the rascals."[17] To someone for whom the experience of suffering negated God's existence, Rahner countered, "Have you even once tried to make your experience of happiness, of meaning, of joy, of shelteredness, likewise an argument from which the presentiment of the eternal God of light and blessedness can unfold in you?"[18]

Despite Rahner's appreciation of the prayer of joy in the world, he prefers to emphasize the negative way because here the human spirit experiences its proper transcendence. As he says, "The experience of the meaning of inner worldly values, in love, in fidelity, in beauty, in truth, and so on is finite. As such these values are a promise in their positive aspect, while in their finiteness they are an indication that we must always proceed beyond these partial experiences, in the hope of this infinite fulfillment."[19]

For Rahner, however, a "burned-out," "tired and disillusioned heart" is not necessarily closer to God than a young and happy one. All too often do both routine, humdrum, daily joys and sorrows obscure God's presence. Nonetheless, because the human mystery is infinite emptiness and the divine mystery infinite fullness, "wherever space is really left by parting, by death, by renunciation, by apparent emptiness, provided the emptiness that cannot remain such is not filled by the world, or activity, or chatter, or the deadly grief of the world—there God is."[20]

Thus God is experienced more clearly and more intensely in our ordinary and banal everyday existence, "where the graspable contours of our everyday realities break and dissolve."[21] To

17. Egan, *Karl Rahner—I Remember*, 84.

18. *Is Christian Life Possible Today?* trans. Salvator Attanasio (Denville, N.J.: Dimension, 1984) 126.

19. Biallowons, Egan, and Imhof, eds. *Karl Rahner in Dialogue*, 152.

20. *Biblical Homilies*, trans. Desmond Forristal and Richard Strachan (New York: Herder & Herder, 1966) 77.

21. Lehmann and Raffelt, "Experiencing the Spirit," 81.

Rahner, God's presence becomes transparent when "the lights which illuminate the tiny islands of our everyday life go out."[22] The best moment, says Rahner, is when everything that props up our life fails. Then we are forced to ask if the inescapable darkness and silence engulfing us is absolute meaninglessness or a blessed night. Pure Rahnerian prayer is surrendering to the blessed night.

The prayer of everyday life can be experienced negatively in the variety of ways in which "we bear the everyday."[23] We must carry "our cross of the everyday—on which alone our self-seeking can completely die because it has to be crucified inconspicuously. . . . If everything in the everyday becomes such dying, everything in the everyday becomes the rising of love."[24] Then one truly prays the everyday.

For example, one may become dissatisfied with one's life, see clearly that things simply do not add up and yet nurture a real Christian hope in an ultimate reconciliation, that Julian of Norwich is correct when she averred that "all will be well." One may try to love God, to pray, but no answer comes. The heart is left empty, devoid of all emotion and meaning. Perhaps for the first time one has not confused the life-force or the self with God but still surrenders to the mysterious darkness. Hence one's heart of hearts does pray and experiences the "wilderness" of the ever-greater God.

They who obey through the inmost fidelity to conscience and not because of external necessity; who deny self and do their duty despite looking foolish in the eyes of others; who stand by their convictions regardless of the cost—they too pray the prayer of daily life.

One could also call the prayer of daily life the prayer of the "unknown saints." Unknown saints so forget themselves "that they suffer the fate of remaining unrecognized by others."[25] These are "people who leave us with the impression that they have spent their whole lives, with all their disappointments and

---

22. Ibid.
23. "The Prayer of the Everyday," this volume, page 46.
24. Ibid.
25. Billowons, Egan, and Imhof, *Karl Rahner in Dialogue*, 57.

absurdities, for the love of neighbor."[26] As Rahner says, "Where selfless love occurs in daily life; where people die devoutly, patiently, and hopeful of an absolute meaning despite all the absurdities of existence; where people do the simplest tasks of their daily life without an egotistical turning in on themselves . . . this is what sainthood means."[27] That is what Rahnerian prayer means.

Even the atheist or agnostic who lives moderately, selflessly, honestly, courageously, and in silent service to others prays the prayer of daily life as an unknown saint. The courageous, total acceptance of life and of oneself, even when everything tangible seems to be collapsing, is perhaps the primary way of praying the prayer of daily life in so-called secular life. Anyone who does so accepts implicitly the holy, silent mystery that fills the emptiness both of oneself and of life. And because Christ's grace supports this hope against hope, the experience is at least anonymously Christian, that is, Christian in fact, if not in name.

Rahner asks, "Why is any kind of radical moral cynicism impossible for a person who has ever discovered his real self? . . . Why does ultimately fidelity not capitulate in the face of death? Why is real moral goodness not afraid of the apparently hopeless futility of all striving?"[28] Because the prayer of daily life implicitly and secretly experiences the God revealed through the life, death, and resurrection of Jesus Christ.

Rahner gives specific examples of the unknown saints in his brief piece, "Why Become or Remain a Jesuit."[29] He says: "I still see around me living in many of my companions a readiness for disinterested service carried out in silence, a readiness for prayer, for abandonment to the incomprehensibility of God, for the calm acceptance of death in whatever form it may come, for total dedication to the following of Christ crucified."[30]

He mentions specifically his friend Alfred Delp, who signed his final vows with chained hands and then went to his death in

26. Ibid.

27. Ibid.

28. Dych, *Foundations of Christian Faith,* 438.

29. *Madonna* [Jesuit Publication in Melbourne, Australia] (April 1987) 11.

30. Ibid.

Berlin for anti-Nazi activity. Rahner finds consolation in the humble work of a Jesuit in India unknown to Indian intellectuals because of his physical work with the poor. Another example of Rahner's unknown saints is a Jesuit student chaplain, beaten by police along with his students but without the satisfaction of considering himself a "revolutionary."

What of a hospital chaplain who works daily with the sick and dying until even death becomes a "dull routine," or the prison chaplain who is appreciated more for the cigarettes he brings than for the gospel he preaches? For Rahner the prayer of everyday life, the prayer of the unknown saint, is made by "one who with difficulty and without any clear evidence of success plods away at the task of awakening in just a few men and women a small spark of faith, of hope and of charity."[31]

The prayer of everyday life is nothing more than the "more excellent way" of love described in 1 Corinthians 13. As St. Paul says, "Love is patient and kind; love is not jealous or boastful; it is not arrogant or rude. Love does not insist on its own way; it is not irritable or resentful; it does not rejoice at wrong, but rejoices in the right. Love bears all things, believes all things, endures all things" (1 Cor 13:4-7).

This love must be the norm against which everything is to be measured. For example, many contemporary Christians cry that there is only one way to be a Christian. Speaking in tongues, charismatic healings, academic theology, the pope, faith and justice, political and liberation theology, the preferential option for the poor, Christian pacifism, mysticism, appearances of Our Lady at Medjugorje, and the like are often touted as the more excellent way.

But as St. Paul says, without love—the prayer of everyday life—these are nothing. They may be the "triggers" that intensify genuine Christian life, but they may also be turned into fads, ideologies, and idols. No Christian need feel obliged to be present at all the rallies, even when they are genuine.

Rahner's theology of the prayer of everyday life challenges everyone to look more closely at what is actually going on in the depths of their daily lives. What is implicit, hidden, anonymous,

31. Ibid.

repressed, or bursting forth from the center of all we do? To Rahner, wherever there is radical self-forgetting for the sake of the other, an absolute letting go, an absolute yielding of everything, surrender to the silent mystery that embraces all life— there is the Spirit of the crucified and risen Christ and the prayer of everyday life.

For these reasons, therefore, I welcome Bruce Gillette's pellucid and accurate translation of Rahner's *Von der Not und dem Segen des Gebetes.* The original English translation seriously distorted both Rahner's language and thought, a misrepresentation which Gillette has rectified by his competence and diligence.

Harvey D. Egan, S.J.
Boston College
30 March 1997

Note on the Translation

In linguistic terms, German is a very "productive" language, that is, it retains the Germanic feature of allowing the virtually limitless formation of lexical items from existing morphemes of the standard German lexicon. This can occur through the arrangement of discrete morphemes into a word, for example, *Welt-an-schau-ung*, or it enables the speaker or writer to express a concept by using a word that usually exists in the standard lexicon in another form, for example, as a verb, noun, or adjective. Thus the verb *verschütten*, usually translated as "to cover over," "to bury," is frequently used in this text in the past passive participle form as a substantive, *die Verschütteten*, "those who have been covered over," "those who have been buried," or, as normally used in this translation, "the rubbled-over." This productivity of the German language gives the speaker the opportunity for tremendous expressivity. This is an important feature of Rahner's written works.

In his writings Rahner pushed the morphology and syntax of standard German to its limits. Herbert Vorgrimler attributes this unique style to Rahner's vast experience with Latin.[1] In German, Rahner creates words that cannot be found in the standard German lexicon, words that are frequently only found in the writings of Rahner. Rahner's stylistic features are important for the proper understanding of his work, particularly as they affect a translation.

Rahner was born in southern Germany and spent most of his life in the same linguistic area in which High German dialects

1. Herbert Vorgrimler, *Understanding Karl Rahner: An Introduction to His Life and Thought*, trans. John Bowden (New York: Crossroad, 1986) 24–7.

were spoken: Baden, Bavaria, and Tirol. One feature of these *spoken* languages that is apparent in this text is the use of redundancy, that is, repetition to add emphasis to the thought being expressed. There are other features that the reader should bear in mind. These fall under two categories: Rahner's text itself and the mode of the translation.

The eight chapters of the book were originally sermons, that is, the spoken word, which Rahner gave during the Lent of 1946 in St. Michael's Church in the heart of Munich. The situation, the date, and the location are important.

Lent is the time in the liturgical year for inner renewal and change of heart. Lent in the center of Munich in March and April of 1946 occurred in the midst of rubble. Munich had been bombed to the ground during the war, and only a few gutted-out buildings, mostly churches, remained standing. There are photographs of postwar Munich that show nothing but broken stone and brick, heaps of rubble over the horizon, just as the devastating bombardment had left them.

This was the first Lent in Munich since the end of the war, the collapse of the Third Reich, and occupation by the United States Army. In early 1946 the CARE packages had not yet started to arrive; the Marshall Plan did not exist; there was little food, potable water, or public utilities (in "The Helper-Spirit" Rahner mentions "the slavery of hunger and need which . . . now prevails"). Rahner's sermons are aimed directly at these people, "the people of today." His reference to the existential philosophy of the time, the "nights in the cellars," and particularly of collapse, rubble, and so forth, must have evoked very real, concrete, even frightening memories in the minds of those present in St. Michael's.

Since it is based on sermons, this text is not as rigorous as some of Rahner's theoretical writings. However, it does contain some typical Rahnerian peculiarities: sentences and paragraphs tend to be very long, and he uses parenthetical comments frequently and sometimes within another parenthetical comment. I have, whenever possible, retained these features in the translation because they are Rahner's style and present his mode of thought. To translate these into "proper" English style might make for easier reading but would change Rahner's own thinking and alter his flow of thought.

Frequently Rahner uses expressions that may sound somewhat stilted to today's reader, but these were well-known to his audience as the current German translations of the Bible, Roman Missal, and other liturgical texts of the period.

Whenever possible I have translated *Mensch* as "man," its primary meaning. Sometimes I have used "human being" or "people" according to the context, but the original is always *Mensch*. I have only used "person" when Rahner used *Person* (for example, "the autonomous person"), because of its use as a technical term. I have also included some biblical references for the convenience of the reader who may not have a concordance at hand. Rahner also makes reference to various philosophers, from ancient to modern. Exact references to those sources are left to the interest of the reader.

One final comment on the text: Rahner considered these sermons as an important work,[2] and one of his editors regards them as Rahner's theoretical work on prayer.[3] They had a profound and lasting effect upon me when I first read them in 1964 while a student at the University of Munich. This fundamental Christian message to the people assembled in St. Michael's in 1946 is just as compelling to the people of today. I hope that the labor of translation has done justice to the spirit of the original text.

My special thanks go to Rev. Harvey Egan, S.J., who kindly reviewed the final draft of the translation and offered many valuable comments and suggestions, particularly on technical terms in theology and Jesuit spirituality. Special thanks also go to Miss Cho Jun Sang and Rev. John Burghard, O.F.M. Conv., without whose support this translation would never have been published.

Bruce W. Gillette
Holy Week of 1997

2. See Vorgrimler, *Understanding Karl Rahner*, 185 n. 2.

3. Karl Rahner, *Gebete des Lebens*, ed. Albert Raffelt (Freiburg i.Br.: Herder, 1984) 206. This book has been translated as *Prayers for a Lifetime* (New York: Crossroad, 1986).

Foreword

These eight short chapters on Christian prayer are not intended to address the theme of prayer in every respect. For the most part, they were originally sermons that were held during Lent of 1946 at St. Michael's Church in Munich, and they bear the traces of this source without the intention of hiding this origin.

If we are not supposed to cease praying, then perhaps one shouldn't cease speaking about prayer, speaking about it as well and as poorly as it is given to one.

Foreword to the Ninth Printing

These little meditations were originally—more than thirty years ago—sermons in Munich at St. Michael's Church. The little book went through many printings, particularly in the Herderbücherei. At the request of the publisher and many readers of the Herderbücherei it is presented again after being out of print for several years. These meditations naturally do not claim to present a systematic theology of prayer. If this were the intention, much would have to be said, particularly today, that is simply presupposed here. And, after so many years, even the author himself would not seldom say differently what is said here even though he still stands behind what he attempted to stammer about prayer then and now.

The book's history of more than thirty years, always with more readers, lets the author hope that it will also find new readers even today. For, as he had written in the first edition, "If we are not supposed to cease praying, then perhaps one shouldn't cease speaking about prayer; speaking about it as well and as poorly as it is given to one."

Karl Rahner, S.J.
Munich, February 1977

1

Opening Our Hearts

Man does very many quite diverse things. He does not have the gift of always doing one thing, although he bears a secret, perhaps unacknowledged and semiconscious longing always to do just one single thing; something that is everything and worth the effort, the heart's final exertion and love. Man must do many things. But not everything he does is of the same order and the same dignity. It can be something "important" because it is unavoidable. And the really important and necessary can be very easily avoided and forgotten. What everyone does, and no one can omit, is not unconditionally the highest priority. When man is with God in awe and love, then he is praying. Then he doesn't perform everything at once, because it will never be possible for him, the finite, to do that in this life. But he is at least with him who is everything, and therefore he does something most important and necessary. Something not everyone does. For just because prayer belongs to the most necessary it is also the freest, the most avoidable, which only exists when we do it freely, always with new love, otherwise it would not exist. However, that's the reason that it seldom happens. It is difficult for man. Therefore he always has to meditate about what prayer is, and he must not wait until it happens by itself. Meditating on the nature and dignity of prayer can cause saying at least one thing to God: Lord, teach us to pray![1]

But don't we all know what prayer is, can't we all pray, can this actually be a matter of something different from the exhortation and admonition to do what we really know and are capable

---

1. Translator's note: Luke 11:1.

1

of doing? That is not so simple and self-evident. Often we really don't know what prayer is, and therefore we often are unable to pray. Because there are human things, acts of the heart, which everyone thinks he knows because everyone talks about them. He knows them because they are obviously very simple. However, the most self-evident and the simplest acts of the heart are the most difficult, and man only learns them slowly. And if he is capable of them at the end of his life, then his life was good, delightful, and blessed. And to these acts of the heart, the simplest and most difficult at the same time, belong goodness, selflessness, love, silence, understanding, true joy—and prayer. No, it's really not easy to know and understand what prayer is. Perhaps at one time someone did know or was capable of it, at a time when his poor heart wasn't yet so worn out by the bitterness and joy of life, just as perhaps he was once capable of pure love. But then gradually something quite unusual came about without his knowing it—just as love can become a habit and perhaps become a mutual egotism—and this human being still thought that he was praying. And then he either gave it up, disappointed and bored, because he slowly noticed that what he was going to do really wasn't worth it anymore. Or he "prayed" on (if one can still call what he continued to do "prayer"). It's like going to a government office. One either has something to pay for or something to pick up, and thus one simply goes there in the name of God. One needs something from one's dear God, and therefore one asks for it. One doesn't want to be on bad terms with him, and one does one's duty. One pays the visit (not too long, what has to be said can truly be said quickly, and surely God too must realize that one doesn't have much time and has more important things to do). And this application at the supreme office of the world's government (one has the impression that it takes a lot of requesting and very slowly functions) and this official visit with the world's supreme ruler, whom one doesn't want to displease (because that could be dangerous in the hereafter, one is never sure), is called prayer. Oh, God, this isn't prayer, but rather the corpse and the lie of a prayer.

But what is prayer actually? That's difficult to say. And in the end we shall have talked a lot about it without having said much. First, let's say something quite simple about prayer, something very self-evident which is at the very beginning of prayer and which we usually overlook: in prayer we *open* our hearts to God. In order to understand that, to understand it with the heart and not just with the head, two things have to be discussed: the rubbled-over heart and the opening of the heart.

The events that occur concretely in our exterior life, clearly and manifestly, are, when one examines them, often only a sign and a symbol, an external shadow of things that take place in the heart, perhaps have been taking place for a long time, and now, without anyone's noticing it, they suddenly form the exterior reality of man according to their hidden nature. And then, in this exterior process and occurrence, man can suddenly look at the secret condition of his heart as in a mirror. And when he sees this, his reflection, and knows that he is actually seeing himself in this external thing, then this shuddering and knowing heart is perhaps frightened to death of itself.

Do you remember the nights in the cellar, the nights of deadly loneliness amidst the harrowing crush of people? The nights of helplessness and of waiting for a senseless death? The nights when the lights went out, when horror and impotence gripped one's heart, when one mimed being courageous and unaffected? When one's innocently bold and brave words sounded so strangely wooden and empty, as if they were already dead before they even reached the other person? When one finally gave up, when one became silent, when one only waited hopelessly for the end, death? Alone, powerless, empty. And if the cellar really became buried by rubble, then the picture of today's man is complete. For such are we people of today, even if we already have crawled out of the rubbled-over cellars, even if our everyday has already begun again, even if one attempts to assume again the pose of the courageous and vivacious one (oh, how fundamentally strange this pose is, this role which we want to play for ourselves and others). We men of today are still the rubbled-over because as such we have already entered into an exterior destiny, because the exterior destiny—by God, it is so even if it sounds so fantastic and romantic—is only the shadow of events which have occurred in the depths of men: that their hearts are rubbled-over.

Say it yourselves: How is our heart? Look at this heart, our heart. If God has not yet really freed it into his own infinite freedom, it is that inward point in our being, where finiteness, agony, hopelessness, the everydayness of our humanity become aware of themselves and consume themselves. That is actually our heart: the heart of fools, the heart of the bitter, the heart of the despaired. We cannot flee this prison of our heart. Man can indeed—literally or figuratively—travel, he can plunge himself into his work, he can devote himself to pleasure, he can attempt to console himself through other people, he can stupefy himself on a thousand paths and in thousands of ways so that he deadens that always silently, pitilessly penetrating consciousness, the consciousness of loneliness, of the inescapability, and the nothingness of the earthly. But this everlasting, hasty, and despaired flight is for naught. Suddenly man notices again that he has not escaped at all, that he is like someone who is seemingly healthy but at the same time incurably ill, who has already heard his death sentence, and in the middle of a pleasant diversion, when the old desire for life and joy is rising as if nothing had happened, he is reminded by a small quiet pain that everything is already over and hopeless. Oh, man can go where he wants, he can create caches of his happiness where he wants, can divert himself over the whole wide world; suddenly he notices again that he was only running around hastily in the dungeon of his life, that he crawled out of one hole in his rubbled-over cellar into another and that everything took place during his imprisonment, that he remains arrested, remains arrested in and to finiteness, to futility, to the everyday, to disappointment, to empty talk, to misery, to the hopeless attempts which we call human life. Certainly there are people who, as it were, sit innocently and without concern in the cellar of the house of their life; they merrily consume their provisions, perhaps they still discuss things excitedly, perhaps they still love and make plans—and they have not yet noticed that the entrance to their cellar has already caved in and is buried under rubble. Caved in because death stands above everything and the end is behind everything. But sooner or later even the "vivacious," "optimistic" man will recognize earthly man's situation. And the others have already noticed what man's situation actually is, man in whom the spirit only appears to be the light to illuminate the hopelessness of the situation as when one lights a match in a cellar to discover that it's hopeless. And when this despair has grasped man, when he notices how lonely he is, how alone, how he is doomed to death and yet still crushed by the vanities of the everyday—oh, then man doesn't need to cry out in despair, then he probably doesn't begin to rave—oh, no, there is a much more horrifying type of despair. When despair has become such a normal condition, so self-evident that one doesn't even know the difference any more, that one doesn't even believe in the possibility of another condition, that one is finished, finished with what one calls the illusions of life, finished with what one still wonders about a bit as childlike ideals and ecstasies but then smiles at somewhat bitterly. People with this chronic despair remain in control of themselves, they remain quite normal and everyday. They conduct themselves as all reasonable people conduct themselves. They do their duty, they work, they are very proper and very conscientious, they fall in love and get married, they pay taxes and discuss art and science, and they like to hear or talk occasionally about the meaning and grandeur of human life. But all that is only a facade. All this is only supposed to cover up the innermost, the deepest point of the heart, the wound of the heart from which one slowly bleeds to death, about which one doesn't talk, however, because of propriety (a proper and educated human being is not supposed to despair). All that should only mask the rubbled-over dungeon of our heart in which the real human being is hopelessly held captive, the human being who knows that everything is finite, everything is pathetic, everything is unimportant, everything that we call our earthly life in us and outside of us is doomed to death. Yes, one has found even a stranger way of masking this despair. One says that it is actually the true greatness of man to despair. Only such a despaired one, who has finished and figured out everything and has noticed that behind everything there is nothing, is the actual, the true man, who has elevated himself above the everyday bourgeois, who bravely and honestly professes the only greatness of man that there is: the honest realization of man's nothingness; the greatness of man is the knowledge of his misery. It can be that such an illusion-free realization is the beginning of salvation, that such men are no longer far from the kingdom of God. Because if they are really so despaired, and they don't make their despair into a perverse pride and imagine (for it's nothing else) themselves, by their own power, to be the despaired emptiness, rather that they are prepared to be the bestowed fullness from the grace of another (the one other). But, as stated, this interpretation of man's nothingness which, if it is comprehended and borne, would constitute his greatness, is often only a guilty masking of despair which neither allows the expression of real despair (because pride deadens it) nor conquers it (because one does not want to let oneself be saved from it). Therefore this masking is no better than its more primitive forms in other men. If one looks at these men and sees through the mask of their despair which has become everyday and cleverly disguised for them and the world, then these men suddenly and mysteriously are transformed into ruins of men, into ruins with facades behind which is the nothing and emptiness, with cellars in which the actual man, the man of freedom, of trust, of faith and infinity, lies rubbled-over and dead.

That is the human heart that has not been freed into the freedom of the infinite God, the rubbled-over heart. And—that is almost the decisive thing for us—we are never delivered from this danger of being rubbled-over, we, the so-called good Christians, faithful to the Church, the ones who "practice the faith." We can continue to live and practice our patented Christianity—and perhaps our heart has been long rubbled-over. Hearts change quietly, and their collapse doesn't make any noise. And they have often changed before we really notice it. And it can happen to us, and perhaps it already has happened—totally or partially—that our heart has become rubbled-over, that the last and innermost chamber of our heart, where we actually are really ourselves, is buried by the rubbish of the everyday, buried by doubt and skepticism, buried by despair and bitterness. One is not protected against this just by continuing to practice the faith. Because even this Christian life can—oh, everything is possible—belong to a facade behind which one hides his deadly sickness from the world and above all from oneself, the sickness unto death,[2] the sickness of secret unbelief, of despair, the paralysis of the interior

---

2. Translator's note: John 11:4 (KJV). "When Jesus heard that, he said, 'This sickness is not unto death, for the glory of God, that the Son of God might be glorified thereby.'"

man who is unable to come out of the prison of this finiteness into the light, into the goodness, into the one, free, boundless, exalted-above-all-death reality of the living God. One can be a Christian, not because one believes but because one wants to hide one's unbelief for and from himself because this would otherwise frighten oneself too much. Indeed, from the nature of the matter, Christianity is the best disguise of unbelief for man's deceived heart, the best facade to hide the rubbled-over heart.

Is the case of the rubbled-over heart hopeless? Is the danger of collapse and being rubbled-over inescapable in the interior man? What can man do if he is supposed to get out of the dungeon of his disguised cold despair and disappointment? How does the opening of one's heart take place? We can say it with one word: by prayer to God and only by prayer. However, precisely because we want to understand what prayer actually is, we have to speak slowly and cautiously. And ask what man has to do when he finds himself in the situation of the rubbled-over heart.

This is the first thing: he must stand firm and submit to it. When people notice that they are rubbled-over spiritually, then they begin either to defend themselves with the despair of one drowning—just like one buried alive. They plunge into everything, into every form of activity and busyness that gives them the hope that in this way they can delude themselves about their despair. Or they really despair, wildly or in icy calm. They curse, they hate themselves and the world and say there is no God. They say there is no God because they confuse the true God with what they held to be their God. And they are actually right in their opinion. The God that they meant really does not exist. The God of earthly security, the God who saves one from life's disappointments, the God of life's assurance,[3] the God who makes sure that children never cry and that justice enters upon the earth to change the misery of this earth, the God who doesn't let human love end in disappointment. But even this second type of man can't stand firm against despair. They think that they have courageously and honestly drawn the right consequence from their experience of life, but they didn't understand despair correctly, for they saw in it the death of God and not his true advent. No, it is

3. Translator's note: *Lebensversicherung* also means life insurance.

really true. In this occurrence in the heart, let despair take every-thing away from you,[4] in truth you will only lose the finite and the futile, no matter how great and wonderful it was, even if it is you yourself. You yourself with your ideals, you yourself with your life's calculations which were very intelligently, very exactly, and very beautifully ordered, you with your image of God which resembled you instead of the Incomprehensible himself. Whatever can be taken from you is never God. Let all your exits be blocked, only the exits to the finite will be rubbled-over and the ways into the really futile. Don't be afraid of the loneliness and isolation of your inward jail which only seems to be filled with feebleness and hopelessness, with tiredness and emptiness! Don't be afraid![5]

You see, when you stand firm and don't flee despair, nor in despairing of your former gods—the vital or the intellectual, the beautiful and the respectable, oh, yes, that they are—which you called God, if you don't despair in the true God, if you stand firm—oh, that is already a miracle of grace which shall be be-stowed on you—then you suddenly will become aware that in truth you are not at all rubbled-over, that your jail is closed only to empty finiteness, that its deadly emptiness is only the false ap-pearance of God, that his silence, the eerie stillness, is filled by the Word without words, by him who is above all names, by him who is everything in everything. And his silence tells you that he is there.

And that is the second thing that you should do in your de-spair: notice that he is there, know that he is with you. Become aware that he has been expecting you for quite some time in the deepest dungeon of your rubbled-over heart. Become aware that he has been quietly listening for a long time whether you, after all the busy noise of your life, and all the idle talk that you called your illusion-free philosophy of life, or perhaps even your prayer during which you only talked to yourself, after all the despaired weeping and mute groaning about the need of your life, whether

4. Translator's note: From here to the end of the chapter Rahner uses the familiar form of the second-person pronoun, i.e., *du, dein,* etc.

5. Translator's note: Cf. Matt 17:7 in the Gospel of the second Sunday of Lent and Isaiah 43:1: "Fear not, for I have redeemed you!"

you finally could be silent before him and let him speak the word, the word that seemed only to be like a deadly silence to the earlier man who was you. You should feel that you are not falling at all when you give up the frantically violent interior anxiety about yourself and your life. You do not despair at all when you doubt yourself, your wisdom, your strength, your ability to help yourself to life and the freedom of happiness; rather, you are with him suddenly as a miracle that daily has to happen anew and never can become a routine. Suddenly you will experience that the petrifying visage of hopelessness is only God's rising in your soul, that the darkness of the world is nothing but God's radiance which has no shadow, that the apparent waylessness is only the immensity of God who does not need any ways because he is already there. Then you will notice that he actually does not have to enter your rubbled-over heart, rather that you have to comprehend that you should not try to escape from this heart because he indeed is there, and so there can be no reason to flee from this blessed despair to a consolation which would be none and which does not exist. Then you will notice that you have to enter—the free yes of your faith and your love—your rubbled-over heart in order to find there the one who was always there and was waiting, the true, the living God. That is the second thing. He is there. He is in the middle of your rubbled-over heart. He alone. He who is everything and, therefore, looks as if he were nothing. He is there not although but because you otherwise have nothing more, not even yourself.

And then the third and fourth things come by themselves. Then tranquillity comes by itself. Stillness which no longer goes away. Trust which no longer fears. Security which no longer needs assurance. Power which is mighty in impotence. Life which unfolds into death. Then nothing more is in us than he and the faith which is sheerly imperceptible but fills everything and conquers everything and holds everything fast, that he is, is there, and we are his. And then tranquillity of heart is found.

And then our heart begins to speak as if by itself. Quietly and without many words. And then it speaks to God who is in us, who holds us although we are falling, who strengthens us although we are weak, who is near to us although we cannot touch him. Our heart speaks to him. What does it say anyway? Who can say it? This heart says itself. And therefore no man can actually say what it speaks because one cannot turn a heart into words. It says to its God: "Thou!" Respectfully, but intimately. And when it speaks, all the strength of this heart flows to this present God, and it does not come back. And man forgets himself. And he no longer has his center in himself, but in God, up there, but for the first time really in himself, because God is more interior to us than we are to ourselves. And all the incomprehensibilities of this God spur on with this God even more the risk of jumping over all the walls of one's own I. For one now knows: There is no salvation inside of these walls, and the more inscrutable his ways, the more devastating his judgments, all the greater is the holy defiance of this heart's love that flees from God's judgment and devastating act in this world to him himself. This God is there, there in the heart of consoled despair, and this heart opening itself says to him: "My God and my Lord, my God and my share in eternity." It says to him: "Abba, dear Father." It prays to him: "Our Father . . . ." It says to him: "Amen." It says to him: "Have mercy on us." It opens itself to him, gives itself, surrenders unconditionally, it listens to his wordless speaking, it trembles in the incomprehensibility of his presence in a pain which would be deadly if it were not the healing pain of eternal love. And everything that the rubbled-over and therein freed heart does and experiences: standing firm and submitting to despair, the consciousness of the rising of God in the fall of man, the tranquillity and the words of love to God, all of these are the actual words, that is his prayer.

Such action, as the Son did it, is grace when we imitate him. One cannot actually show someone how to do it. One cannot force someone to let go of the plank one is frantically clinging to although he knows that it cannot save him, the plank of despaired self-assertion and of self-asserting despair. How little use it is to tell someone: You can swim, you won't fall, when he desperately protests that he cannot do it, that he is falling. One can only say one thing to him: the grace of ability comes in the form of your freedom. It is no guarantee that eliminates the need to jump by already convincing you forcefully that you won't fall into the bottomless pit when you let go. One can only say: Don't worry about your anxiety which wants to be assured before it lets go, before it prays. If you think your heart cannot pray, then pray with your mouth, kneel down, fold your hands, speak loudly, even if it all seems like a lie to you (it is only the desperate self-defense of your unbelief before its death which is already sealed): "I believe, help my unbelief; I am powerless, blind, dead, but you are mighty, light, and life and have conquered me long ago with the deadly impotence of your Son." One can only say again and again: Your supposed inability with which you excuse your inaction does not precede as a simple fact your willingness, but *is* your deepest guilt, *or*—oh, who has fathomed the mind of the Lord—as long as you crave the ability and are not in love with your inability (are you certain of that, my poor brother?), is the impotence of the Lord which will save you. But even then: Why doesn't your knee, your hand, your mouth want to speak what your heart supposedly cannot? Because it would be dishonest? But is it dishonest to act thus with the body when the heart desires to be able to do what it supposedly is not yet able to do? But don't we agree that your heart should crave what it—as you say—can't do, to believe in meaning, freedom, happiness, breadth, clear truth, in God? How could you express what is in you with the bitter words, "I can't do it," without admitting at the same time that it would be good, is desirable and obligatory to be able to do? I mean that it's a fact that grace comes in the form of your free act; and it is never so that you only have to wait for it. You can always do one thing, while on your knees and with your mouth: shout into the impotent, unbounded darkness of your dead heart's wasteland that you yearn for God; one thing you can do that we all have to do: pray.

One thing still has to be said. This remoteness of God would not be the rising of God in our dead and rubbled-over heart, had not the Son of Man—who is the Son of the Father—suffered and done all of this in his heart with us, for us, and before us. He, however, has suffered and done all of this. It happened in the garden from the fruits of which men wanted to press the oil of joy which, however, was in truth the garden of the lost paradise. He lay face down; death had risen in his heart, in the living heart of the world. Heaven was closed and the world was like a huge grave; he alone was in it, buried by the guilt and hopelessness of the world. The angel who looked like death gave him the chalice of all bitterness for strength, and he fell into agony. The earth swallowed evilly and greedily the drops of the blood from his death-agony. God encompassed everything as a night that no longer promised a day. One could no longer distinguish him from death. In this immeasurable silence of death—the people were sleeping dumbly in sadness—in this deathly silence, the only sign that was still left of God, somewhere the little voice of the Son was floating around. Every moment it seemed ready to be smothered. Then the great miracle occurred: the voice remained. The Son said with this tiny voice—which resembled that of someone dead—to his dreadful God: "Father," he said to his own forsakenness, "your will be done." And, in ineffable courage, he committed his forsaken soul into the hands of this Father.

Since then our poor soul has also been laid in the hands of this God, this Father whose deadly decree became love. Since then our despair is redeemed, the emptiness of our heart has become fulfillment, and the remoteness of God our homeland. *If* we pray with the Son in the tired darkness of our heart and repeat to God his prayer in the garden. In pure faith. No storm of ecstasy will rise up at first when his words mysteriously arise again as our words somewhere in the depth of our heart. But the power will suffice. It will be just enough for each day. As long as it pleases God. And that will be sufficient. He knows when and where our heart will be sufficiently purified (to some extent, it's possible even on earth) to bear the blinding rising of his blessedness, the poor heart that now in faith in Jesus Christ shares *the* night that for our eyes is nothing other than the blinding darkness of the rapturous light of God, the heavenly night when God is born in our heart for the first time.

Oh, we have now talked a lot about prayer but said little. But perhaps it's a start, a very small impetus for a start that we could make anew and originally in prayer? Just hearing the message is naturally not worth anything. But if we people of today would only try it, would try to accept ourselves as we are, to look at our disguised or acknowledged despair, if we, as it were, descended into the depths of our hearts, if we gave up deceiving ourselves about ourselves, if we had the courage to renounce inwardly what life takes from us anyway—namely everything—if we suddenly would notice, after giving up everything, that we possess everything, would notice that he actually is totally with us right now, the silent, nameless, incomprehensible One who is everything, if we would then notice in the loneliness of our rubbled-over heart that this poor heart bears infinity within itself, if we would begin to speak softly: Our Father, you are in the heaven of my heart even when it seems to be a hell; hallowed be your name, may it be called upon in the deadly stillness of my perplexed silence; to us come your kingdom when all abandons us; your will be done even if it kills us because it is life, and what seems like a setting on earth is the rising of your life in heaven; give us this day our daily bread—let us ask for this also that we never mistake ourselves for you, not even in the hour when you are near us, rather, at least by our hunger, we notice that we are poor and unimportant creatures; free us from our guilt and protect us during the temptation of guilt and trial that is actually only one: not believing in you and the incomprehensibility of your love; but deliver us—deliver us from ourselves, deliver us into you, deliver us into your freedom and into your life.

If we were to begin in a similar way, to speak to God with far fewer words and much more heart, I believe that our heart would have opened up, and we would have spoken a word of prayer.

2

The Helper-Spirit

When we open our hearts, when we pause in the harried flight from ourselves, when the appearance of God-forsaken loneliness, which we were fleeing up to now, is mysteriously transformed into the true arrival of God, when we begin to say "our Father" in the stillness of our heart, is it we alone who dare to speak these enormous words to God?[1] Who helps us pray? From where do we get the courage and power to pray?

One thing gives us power. We speak to God in common with his Son, our Lord Jesus Christ. He, who can adore the Father in spirit and in truth because he rests at the Father's heart for all eternity as the only-begotten, has invited us, his brothers in flesh and in spirit, together with him confidently and boldly, to call the eternal, living God of judgment and all incomprehensibility our Father. And so we can speak to God in Christ Jesus and in the Church, the people of the brothers of Christ, without having to die from terror of this daring venture by dust and ashes. Because the Son as the Father's messenger has spoken with us and with the Father as our brother, we can pray. If the Son were not present with his word, indeed as the Word of the Father to us, if he had not prayed on our mountains and in our valleys, with our exultation and with our tears, then we would always have to fear that our word of prayer would be swallowed by the silent incomprehensibility above and around us which we would be unable to give a name to. But now we can say confidently, our

---

1. Translator's note: Cf. "We dare to say: Our Father," etc., in the liturgy of the Mass.

Father, because we say it with Jesus. And this childlike Abba—dear Father—is unspeakably much more true than all the metaphysics about God that brings man into the "proper" distance from God; whose love in the Son and in the holy community of his brothers, however, has long ago transcended the infinite distance between him and us and taken us to his heart. Our first prayer aid is that prayer happens with Christ in the Church.

But that's not all. We pray in the Spirit of God. And we want to consider that more closely. We want to say two things. First, there must be a place in our heart for the Holy Spirit of God. Second, this Spirit prays in us and with us.

When we say there must be room in our heart for the Holy Spirit of God, then we mean two things in one. In our inner man there is something like a space for this Spirit itself, not just for a thought or an idea of him, there is a space there even if we don't notice it much. And he is direly needed by us in this space of inward man.

It has gone strangely with man in the recent decades of European intellectual history. Man considers himself to be free, unbound, limitless, only responsible to himself and the inner law of his nature, to be the autonomous person. He wanted to be free and struggled[2] passionately against the tutelage of Church, state, society, convention, morals. He struggled for free science, for free love, for free economics, for freedom of thought, freedom of the press, freedom of association, and a thousand other freedoms. And it was often a great, honest struggle—and sometimes a foolish protest that mistook licentiousness and unrestraint, the freedom of error and ruin, for true freedom. And while man was still raising the battle cry of freedom, this European man suddenly had fallen into a very odd slavery. I do not mean the external coercive system of the past years. I also do not mean the slavery of hunger and need which followed and now prevails. I mean another type of slavery: Autonomous man fell into slavery from *within*. In midst of the innermost core of

---

2. Translator's note: The German words used here and later are *Kampf* and *kämpfen* (struggle, battle, fight, combat). They are also military terms which were very common during World War II; this could also be an allusion to Hitler's book, *Mein Kampf.*

unbound, Church- and dogma-free man, a force arose unexpectedly that beset and enslaved this seemingly completely free man. To the extent that he had removed himself from the exterior ties of universally obligatory morals, obligatory principles of thought and action, to that extent he actually did not become free but fell prey to other powers that conquered him from within. The powers of desire, the powers of egotism, the hunger for power, the powers of sexuality and pleasure and simultaneously the impotence caused by worry which undermines man from within, by insecurity, by loss of life's meaning, by anxiety and futile disappointment. Then there were odd events again. Man, who was occupied in the struggle for his right and freedom, unavoidably had to consider himself very important in this business. In his own eyes he became ever more valuable and significant. And thus his own interior life—and that is the space where he could hope to be the single one—became the object of an ever more radical self-assertion, of an ever more burning compulsion for research, and of an ever more ardent love. However, the deeper he delved into this, the bolder his expeditions through the unknown lands of interior man, the more relentlessly he sought to fathom the secrets of the heart in science, art, and literature, the more questionable everything he found there became. He wanted to discover himself completely and in himself the autonomous person of unimpeachable dignity, but he only discovered—after all the depth psychology and psychotherapy, and all the existential philosophy, and all the anthropology in which all the sciences were involved in order to define what man actually is in his deepest bases and substrata—he only discovered that in the deepest depths of his own being that he is actually not at all himself but a vast, monstrous chaos of each and every thing in which man is only something like a very accidental point of intersection of dark, impersonal drives which come from race and nation or from the sum of hereditary factors or from a collective soul or from the nothing—why not?—they encounter each other mysteriously for a moment and flow through man like a tube from unknown to unknown and without control. And what remains of the I, of the proud, splendid, individual I, that only resembles a cork being driven around without destination on an enormous ocean by dark, nameless, blind forces? Does today's man on his own really know more about himself than that he is a question into a limitless darkness, a question that only knows that the burden of questionability is more bitter than man can bear in the long run?

But this occupation with the depths of human nature did indeed bring out *one* positive result even if it has become a trip into the boundless and dark unchartered. It showed man the expanse of his inner being. What rational, enlightened man at the end of the nineteenth century knew about himself with his shallow philistine education had been so simple: a little bit of body and a lot of ingenuity and reason that can figure out anything because there is natural science and engineering, and all metaphysics would gradually evaporate like the morning fog before the sun which enlightens everything. In all cases, clear, scientific concepts and certainly no mystery, no mysticism, and no delirium. And the soul, at any rate, is not deeper than what the shallowest brain can plumb. And whatever appeared to be a morass or a chaotic abyss in the land of the soul seemed to go away by itself by means of a lot of enlightenment, a little bit of morals, and a good police force. Now, however, it's become different. (For some at least. This hasn't spread around everywhere yet.) One has noticed again that on the proscenium of human consciousness where the performance is in the daylight, only a small part appears that belongs to the soul. One begins to sense that there are hidden depths of the soul to which even one oneself doesn't have free access but which still belong to one: hidden depths in which demons can house, immense expanses and caves filled with mysterious spiritual realities of which each is only the foreground for something still more enigmatic, which only appears to be the reflex for something ungraspable in itself, depths and abysses in which, hidden and almost incalculable, that what man would like to consider his own history of life, based solely on his own personal decision, is being played out before one by mysterious powers. An ancient philosopher[3] said that the soul is in a certain way everything. And we have experienced and suffered this ancient truth anew: man who justified himself in himself has broken into the immeasurable abysses of his soul.

3. Translator's note: Aristotle; cf. *De Anima* III 7. 431^b 20.

But with all that, man has become undefinable. He is puzzling to himself. He finds in himself a maze of impulses and possibilities, and he doesn't know which is the decisive one. What should he consider himself to be? Which of the powers in the depths of his nature should he place on the altars of his heart as his God? Pleasure or power, the instinct of the herd or of isolation, the all-knowing but so impotent intellectuality, exuberant vitality, the knowledge of finiteness that unmasks everything and bears everything without hope? Or what? All are possibilities of the soul, idols of yesterday and tomorrow, all that is in the soul because in its abysses the infinite has room. What should the soul connect itself to, what of this should it make into its own nature from which everything else receives measure and direction? Or should it let itself be driven aimlessly through all the possibilities in order to experience possibly "everything"? But we have already shown that everything escapes one in this way, that this way is only the gleaming mask of cowardice and capitulation to chaos and the flight from what "also" is: from the responsibility of deciding and selecting. No, one can't practice polytheism before the altars of the heart, polytheism that has idols set up and dethroned continually by another as itself. There are many infinities in the soul but not all are God who may be worshiped; but, other than this one, all these infinities are only there to worship, not to be worshiped. They are only those infinities without which man could not call to the truly Infinite. They are not there so that man could enjoy himself as God. How could they be allowed to be that since they are many and thus show themselves as finite? We are not allowed to practice idolatry with the immeasurable expanses of the soul. Therefore where is God, the true God of our heart? But let's first ask: Has everything in these infinite spaces of the soul been uncovered by our experiences? Has the true and secret God really been discovered in the infinite expanses of the heart? Has the holy image of God remained rubbled-over in the depths while all the depth research has only unearthed the rubble of the soul or its preliminaries?

If we want to answer this question, we have to make a statement from the word of God. There is still something quite different in the soul from what everyday experience, existential philosophy or depth psychology or mysticism of nature, of art, or of love, in short, all human attempts to conquer the absolute, have brought to light out of these abysses. When all attempts to dig out of the ground of the heart the all-important, the all-encompassing, the permanent, the godly, have failed, and it always turns out in the end that what has been found is man who cannot worship himself in the long run because this god is too paltry, then the word of God quietly and surely says to this disappointed and despaired treasure hunter: Deep in the abysses of man, God lives nevertheless, the living God, really he himself, not an idol, not just an image of ourselves, but he himself, the living God, the infinite God, the holy God, he who is not just infinity in itself but wants to give us freely his own infinite expanse, that infinity which not only frees us from the enslaving force of the human powers of the soul (which, in themselves finite, only deceive about an infinity in their starving insatiability) but also raises us above the paltry measures of a harmonious humanism in which everything is so formed that it becomes narrow; it also raises us above the single infinity that man can claim for himself with a bit of the appearance of truth: the infinity of his impotence and his finiteness. God is in us. Not just the eternal Thou that saves us from suffocating loneliness, which surrounds the heart, not just that, although even that would be enough for splendor and happiness. He is—dare we say it without the swindle[4] of God-equality grasping us, are we allowed to say it while we all prostrate ourselves before him in the dust of our radical difference from him in order to worship him alone, are we allowed to say that he not only is in us as the liberating Thou but also as that one without whom we cannot comprehend ourselves totally, our own I, as it is really supposed to be and we have not comprehended, as that one who is on our side when we look over and shout to him, as that one who, remaining entirely free and entirely himself, has become in merciful grace with his own reality with his "uncreated grace" that in us from which we alone can comprehend what we are: participating in God's nature through the gracious possession of God's being and life itself? He is in us because he bore witness of it to us through his Word. And this God who lives in us as true infinity for man is called in the word

4. Translator's note: *Schwindel* can also mean dizziness, vertigo, etc.

of Scripture: *the Holy Spirit.* The Spirit of God has been given into our heart. He searches and fills the depths of our heart. He has been poured torrentially into us. He is the anointing and the seal of inner man. He is the fulfillment of all the bottomless abysses of our nature. He is the first fruit and pledge of eternal life. He is the life in us through which we have escaped death. He is happiness without limits that has caused the source of the brooks of our tears to dry up even if they are still flooding the flatland of our everyday experience. He is the inward God, the holiness of the heart, its hidden exultation, its power that wonderfully is still there when we are at the end of our wits and strength. He is in us so that we actually know deep inside, although we are blind fools, for he knows, and he is ours. He it is who loves in us, loves squanderingly, loves exultingly, loves, not egotistically desiring. And this love is ours for he is the eternal love of God, and he is ours, he is our love although we have cold, narrow, petty hearts! He is the eternal youth in the despairful senility of our time and of our hearts. He is laughter that starts to sound quietly behind our weeping. He is the confidence that bears us up. He is freedom, he is the buoyant bliss of our soul.

"Those are splendid words—if they are true," some of you are thinking. "But *I* don't notice any of that, none of that is in me." Who is this I that notices nothing and is devoid of this Spirit? This I does not exist at all, the I that doesn't have *more* in it than what even the outermost surface of our nature, that we usually call our consciousness, can oversee. This I is an abstraction of the Enlightenment's philistine of the nineteenth century. Who am "I" then? I am in truth the man of infinite possibilities, enormous abysses, incalculable expanses! And "I" haven't even wandered through all the lands of my true I. Up to now I only sat in the small, stuffy porter's room of the palace of my heart while in its high and actual chambers eternal happiness and eternal destiny are being lived and decided by me myself. Oh, if the masters and charlatans of knowledge about the depth of the soul are bringing up, like deep-sea divers, hidden splendors and abominations from the deep levels of inward man, if suddenly like psychic earthquakes and dislocations, underground forces like volcanoes break forth on the surface of humanity, volcanoes of demonic hate with all-annihilating lava streams of ruin and destruction—no, then it's settled that the soul can contain more in itself than we happen to notice between getting up in the morning and breakfast. Then, however, it is the shocking glad tidings of our faith for which our little faith is the only thing that hinders us from believing ourselves to be great and infinite. It is the glad tidings of exulting happiness: In the depths of the soul, not only demons of the night, of greed and hate, are housing, where not only the groundwaters of bitterness are flowing of which only a few drops appear in the eyes, not only the abyss of all-devouring skepticism is there. No, still deeper than all that, still more mighty than all that, the Holy Spirit is there, adored and blessed in eternity. And only a quiet, shy, and faithful yes, and then this deepest in the depths, this abyss of the Godhead in the abysses of the soul is mine. He is always there. But he is mine only when I say yes in faith. When I say this yes, whether in blessed exultation or with the last effort of the heart, when the mouth's word seems to precede the word of the heart, then this yes is the grace of the Holy Spirit. But that doesn't give me any right to be silent and say to him: you speak. I must not want to hear his word while being silent, but rather I must say my word so that I hear his word, my word unconditionally and faithfully. If I do it, then the innermost center of my being is no longer an inconceivable something that aimlessly is chased painfully through all the possibilities of undefinable man; but rather it is made fast in God, and his true, incomprehensible infinity beyond my false infinities is mine. How this is possible, only he knows. But have we grasped our true being when we have become so incomprehensible to ourselves as he himself is?

But we're supposed to talk about prayer! We started to do it some time ago. This Spirit of God in the most human part of man, in his heart, this Holy Spirit, deeper than all abysmal wickedness, this strong Spirit that dwells behind all of our weakness, prays in us. He steps in for us with ineffable groans. He is not only God before whom we kneel, he works in us, with us, for us. And most of all when we carry out the decisive part of our life, prayer. As our heart is deeper than the day, so is our prayer deeper than the childishly simple thought that goes through our arid brain, more splendid than the paltry feeling that is like a small moss vegetating miserably on the hard-trampled earth of our heart. When we pray, then the words of prayer rise up like eagles, and they fly with the wings of the Holy Spirit through the endlessness of the land of God without tiring to where he is entirely himself and his heart. *If* we pray. If we pray, then what we say and what we notice in our so-called I is only like the last echo, coming from an immeasurable distance, of the shouting in which God calls himself, of the exultation in which God himself is blissful about the splendor of his infinity, of the self-assertion with which the unconditional founds itself in itself from eternity to eternity.

Oh man, recognize the dignity of your prayer! When you confess that you have become partaker of the divine nature, then you also confess that your prayer is not just the prayer of man, man who is in you, but rather the prayer of the Spirit of God in you. You yourself still don't notice what enormous things are taking place in the abysses of your heart, when you begin to say "our Father." That still sounds poor, helpless, thin and perhaps even presumptuous. It still may seem to you that the little bit of heart that you have experienced in yourself won't cooperate. But in truth, it is quite different. When the Spirit of God is in you, and he is that—or aren't we the baptized who confess Christ in faith and love? Then he speaks in us. And when you listen more closely (Oh, don't listen, but pray, only that alone is now important. You will have an eternity of time to listen; you have, however, only *one* time to pray), then you also perceive something like a sweet, quiet, distant melody that comes forth from those depths where the actual soul sings along with the choirs of eternity and speaks along with the word of eternal love so that one cannot say whether the bride speaks or the Spirit. We don't know what we should ask for. He, however, knows, and that is enough. The shout of our heart seems to die away in the deathly stillness of the God who is silent, unheard. He, however, shouts safely and perceptibly over the abysses of the nothing that separates us from the Eternal. And that is enough. When the searcher of the last depth of the soul searches through our hearts, completely goes through every bit of our heart, oh, then we are not afraid! He won't find our emptiness, nor the mysterious demons of the depth, nor the myriad of masks with which we continually deceive ourselves so that we in the end don't even know who we are. He will find his Holy Spirit. When he listens to the beat of our heart, he doesn't hear the endlessly empty prattle in the marketplace of our heart, nor the uncanny grating of the chained titans in the dungeons of the interior, he hears the unspeakable groaning of his own Spirit who intercedes with God for his holy ones. He hears it as *our* groaning, as those sounds that come from the chaotic dissonances of our heart and life and form a hundred-voiced symphony to the praise of the Most High.

The Spirit is our helper in prayer. If we become tired in prayer, he doesn't. If we are overcome by a boundless aversion to the hollowness of our heart and our prayer, he remains blissful in the always morning-like freshness of exultation with which he praises the Father. If we become frightened about the secret unbelief that seems to kill the words of prayer like a deadly poison before they are quite out of the heart, he speaks the words that no longer believe because they themselves are already the believed in view. If the secret hopelessness of the heart struggles in our prayer with the confidence of the words of prayer that often seem to be so artificial even to ourselves, he prays in us himself, the unshakable certainty of the eternal God. If our word to God, I love you, often sounds so forced from our heart that the eerie danger seems to be lurking that the forced fulfillment of the duty of love could suddenly change into the insane hate of someone whom one *must* love, he prays in us and with us the song of songs of love that is only pure, flowing ecstasy about the beloved God beyond all obligation and all law. He prays in us when we pray. The Spirit is a helper in our prayer, not in the sense that he only helps for what *we* experience as our prayer in us but rather in the sense that our prayer is infinitely more than our prayer because he helps. Because he helps, our prayer is a piece of the melody that rushes through the heavens, an aroma of incense that sweetly rises to the eternal altars of heaven before the triune God. The Spirit of God prays in us. That is the holiest consolation in our prayer. The Spirit of God prays in us. That is the most exalted dignity of our prayer. The Spirit of God prays in us when we join in with his prayer. That gives us a new—but also blessed—duty and responsibility to really pray now and not to slacken. He prays in us. That is the power of prayer that never fails. He prays in us. That is the inexhaustible content of all our prayer that flows from the empty cisterns of our heart. He prays in us. That will be the fruit of eternity from the prayers of this time.

Our prayer is to a certain extent consecrated by the Holy Spirit. Let's pause before we begin to pray. And when inner man has come to rest, when everything is quiet, and in this silence all the essential powers freely and softly coalesce, and the waters of grace silently rise out of the spring of the depth according to holy law and quench that in our prayer which our spirit and will do, then we want to let the Spirit of the Father and the Son speak. We don't hear him. But we know in faith that he prays in us, prays with us and for us. And that his word echoes in the depths of our heart and in the heart of the eternal Father. We let the Spirit pray. And in trembling awe and in sweet love, we repeat his word to him. We pray.

3

The Prayer of Love

Love of God and prayer both pose a mutual difficulty for us. They both belong to acts of the heart which really only succeed when one forgets to *whom* one offers them—namely God—and forgets that one is doing them, which usually, or even necessarily, fails when one tries to make sure that one is doing it correctly. One can reflect upon it afterwards, and this may even be good. One can reflect on love and prayer and attempt to describe what takes place during them. However, examination by reflection somehow is always the death of the act itself (just as one cannot disassemble a rifle for inspection and shoot it at the same time). One can only know whether the noble act of the heart really succeeds when one does it and forgets what one is doing. Indeed, it can be—and this danger is particularly great for us people of today—that someone becomes so stuck in the deadly cycle of reflection about oneself that he becomes almost incapable of the real acts that are directed to God. Instead of being with *God* in knowledge and love, he is only with his own knowing and feeling relative to God. He no longer, so to speak, tastes the quality of his object, but only that of his act, and he finds himself hopelessly imprisoned in his "subjectivity," which he correctly holds to be problematic, poor, and ambiguous. He thinks even the loftiest uplifting of his spirit would remain powerlessly entangled in dark images and parables of which one would never know whether they are really the shadow of the intended object or only that of one's own vacuous desires. Man can no longer escape himself. The path of his acts takes an unusual turn and ends—to his nameless despair—with himself, with his thoughts and feelings, instead of through them with that One whom they actually intend. Then we consider our thoughts and feelings not according to the object at which they are directed but rather, as it were, in themselves alone and find them indeed wanting and very unreal. We don't want to consider this self-consuming reflection, how it arises and how one could escape it, why its petrifying impression in the end is indeed false, why this jail of a rubbled-over heart, without our noticing it, indeed although we often don't want to admit it, has been open for a long time.

Something else should be explained by this danger. Because we instinctively seek to avoid this danger of deadening reflection, today we easily end up in another. We think it would be best to avoid such acts of directly viewing God in love and knowledge, honoring the Inscrutable in silence (even in silence before ourselves!), not even trying to give the Inexpressible a name, not wanting to look at *him*, rather to let him look at *us*, that is, at our selfless work on earth, at our silent goodness toward our fellow man, at our inner decency, at the discreet patience with which we bear the incomprehensibility of our existence. In our relationship with God, we feel as if he is with us, as it were, silently standing behind us, just as long as we don't say his name, don't turn around so that he won't disappear the moment when we do. The dread of deadly reflection causes the temptation of wanting to be irreligious, or better, only anonymously religious, and these people suspect—naively and conceitedly at the same time—unaffectedly and expressly religious people of mistaking God for their thoughts and feelings about God. And when someone falls prey to this temptation of devout irreligiosity, he naturally rejects prayer and such a thing as the explicit expression of his love for God in prayer.

But when we recognize the ground on which this anxiety of explicit religiosity grows, when we see that it is the anxiety of reflex that omits the act toward God because he fears to end up with himself instead of with God, because he would only be ready to deal with the Infinite if its infinity would show itself to him directly in its own self, because he refuses to be with God patiently in the manner which is required of us in the preliminarity of this life: in the unity of the retained sign and of the reference of the sign beyond itself. Then we can see again that the ancients were indeed correct when they explained that the objective relationship between God and man requires that man look at God himself in knowledge, acknowledgment, faith, worship, hope, and love and not just indirectly and inclusively honor him through acts that directly relate to something else. For God is recognizable from his works (even if only as the Incomprehensible above all his works), God has spoken to us in his Son (even if the latter could only speak of his Father in human words), God has given his Spirit into our hearts (even if we only know about it for certain because the Son told us). How could we not raise our eyes to him himself, open our heart and mouth in order to confess him—expressly and openly—give him honor, dare to address him, to say "Thou" and "Father" to him? Indeed, in such action, he is only "there" for us when the act of the spirit and the heart always, as it were, goes out into the unknown, uncertain, and inscrutable, beyond what it knows of him and loves, when it aims at what it will never reach (as long as we are far from the Lord on our pilgrimage and the Spirit given into our heart remains the hidden God). But is this a reason to omit such acts or rather the explanation why all such acts remain faith and that in the formal structure of such acts is the introduction for what really counts in the end: that man dare to leap, as it were, away from himself (even if he only can arrive at the goal when the eternal light enlightens him)? Would we think we would be closer to God if he remained the nameless, unnamed beyond all things with which alone we would have to deal, the eternally unexplained remainder of all our calculations (however, with which we would not be able to reckon)? But then this imageless religion would have soon evaporated into atheism. The mystery must be named, called to, loved, so that it remains here for us—it is always going to remain a mystery anyway.

Every uplifting of the heart which intends this God himself directly, is prayer. And the pure fullness of this prayer, in which man accomplishes everything at once that is possible in reference to God, is called loving as a Christian. The commandment of love is the fullness not only of the law but also of prayer. In this prayer man no longer says something conditional or limited: a petition to God, a confession of his guilt, a glorifying confession of God's attributes. He says himself by giving himself over to

God, loves himself away to him, as man may only lose himself to God. And therefore man expresses in such prayer also the highest that he is able to say positively about him. He is the one who solely is worthy to be loved with all our strength, unreservedly, unconditionally, and eternally. If the fullness of prayer is love, then we must talk about the love of God if we want to say what prayer is.

But what is the love of God, and how do we find it so that we can pray it? One often says that love shows itself particularly in the observation of the commandments. That's true. But the love of God himself is something different from the observation of his commandments, so much so that without it, all fulfillment of the law is of no use. Thus we justly ask what the love of God itself is. Therefore men try again and again, as well or as poorly as it happens to go, to describe what is occurring in the heart of man when it loves its God. And even if it is true that they who know how to talk about it do not necessarily have more love, so it is also true when someone notices in fright that he probably only has a little love for God when he hears someone else saying things about love that he can only discover with difficulty in his own heart.

Then what is the love of God? We can try to begin from our human experience (even the word of God has to use human words and concepts if it wants to talk about its mysteries) and simply say: What happened in a soul when it loved a human being selflessly and purely? This love should be transferred to God, only let it be more inner, more selfless, more unconditional, let it correspond even more to the one who is being loved here: God!

Much occurs between human beings that is called love. So we must try to say what is meant here. Narrow, egoistic sexual desire is certainly not meant here. For this is in man, at most a lower, not fully developed form of the love meant here, even when it does not mutate into a wanton or brutal drive. And nevertheless this love may not be thought of as simply a good-natured and boring well-wishing that is "selfless" only because it is basically unconcerned. No, love is passionate, but passionate in that impulse of the whole of man (of spiritual man, however, where "spirit" means the innermost of the whole man) to burst the narrow, egoistic sphere, to squander himself (even if it's only his poverty) on the higher that we are not, to forget himself because the other, the better has alone become important. Here we want to talk about this selfless love of the spirit for a human being. It is unselfish rapture of the soul over the beloved human being. It is movement of the heart to the beloved. Man loses himself in the beloved in that blessed self-oblivion of the spirit which overcomes man when in love all his being all at once breaks through the stiff walls of his uneasy self-assertion that encloses him in the narrowness of his own poor nature and pours forth into the other one in order to belong entirely to that one. Forgetting itself, this love clings to the beloved, wants him to be well, and is blessed in his happiness. And strangely, whoever loves this way truly loves the other, he has escaped from the dungeon of his narrowness and not fallen into another one. Not only the value of the beloved being is clear to him in this movement of love to the other unique human being, but also the whole world in its mysterious, blessed depth. Or perhaps more correctly: When a human being moves so lovingly from himself over to another, then "image and parable" of that love which craves everything—God—is already in such love. Whether two human beings who love each other experience the most radical pain or supreme bliss in this love depends on whether they understand that another entirely different love is coming to light in their love; whether they crave God together and meet themselves there. But be that as it may with this puzzling "more" that lives in true love from one human being to another. When we speak of love, let us think of that mysterious pouring out of one's own being into the beloved thou. And then man notices that the daring risk of his love was not in vain, he senses how the answer comes from above, how he also is loved, how love and understanding accept and encompass reverently and tenderly his entire given-away being, how he is better protected in the love of the other than when he still belonged to himself. Active doing of good, faithful care, and self-sacrificing service then bloom as if from themselves out of this unity of love of two hearts as protection and testimony of this hidden love.

If man would only cling to his God with such love! If he finds him, the sublime, holy God, he is beyond all limitations and all comprehension! If he opens himself in love before him, forgets himself, lets go of himself, lets all of his being sink into his God in that highest painful-sweet desire that thoroughly pervades man, if he loses himself and everything in his God! Oh, my God, if man being totally devoted to you may become wholly tender, if he didn't need to be hard and unapproachable, if the holy shame and fear of his soul could fade away in order to show its utmost before you and confess itself and everything that it has and does in bitterness and bliss into your beloved heart! Then it can give itself away as a gift without fear of being deceived, squander its most delightful and deepest part without fear that the blessed exuberance of the loving heart could be changed into the ineffable desolation and bitterness of a deceived heart, of a disappointed love. This love calls to God in the middle of his heart, all the powers of this soul flow toward him in order no longer to return to itself. They flow to him who in love becomes the innermost core of our being, closer to us than we ourselves, more loved than we ourselves, loved not for us but rather for him. And this love of God is pervaded by the happy knowledge that he loved first and always answers to the call of love that urges itself to his heart from the valley of transitoriness and death. This love of God is selfless. It doesn't think of itself, it is faithful and tender, it loves God, not his reward, because it is itself reward enough. It stands firm in cheerless hours, it conquers all bitterness, the waters of distress are not able to extinguish it. It is still and not given to many words because great love is pure and chaste. It is bold and intimate and yet respectful, it despises coarse familiarity before the incomprehensible God because it is not love of just anyone but love of God. Because love is a clinging to another, a self-surrendering to another, therefore all nobility and also all ineffable disgrace of this highest and ultimate thing that a heart is capable of doing comes from that *which* one loves. Therefore love of *God* is so holy and great; therefore it can never cease.

For this love is for God, him, the Infinite, the Incomprehensible, the God near to our heart, the Holy, the Adored. We love Him, before whose Spirit we stand from eternity to eternity, who knows everyone by name, him, our Creator and Lord, our beginning and our end, the infinite Father and Son and Holy

Spirit, the one God. We love him who loved us first, who gave us existence and life, in whom we love, move, and are, him, who loves us continually even when we hate him who even lets his sun rise over our sins, him, the Patient, Faithful, Wise, the God of our heart and our share in eternity, him, the sole Good. The farther his infinity from our nothingness, the more it challenges the boldness of our love. The more complete the dependence of our questionable being on his inscrutable decisions, the more unconditional is the shuddering entrusting of one's one being to the beloved God. The more rapturous his holy beauty and goodness, the more his love transcends everything that we might otherwise call love. The more he visits us with his grace-filled, deifying nearness, the more he is father and mother and brother and sister for us, all the more intimate the holy tenderness of our love will become. The more destructive the incomprehensibility of his ways and judgments, the greater the holy defiance of our love which loves God all the more stronger the more it comprehends him, the more burning the feeling of our blind impotence before God penetrates the last fibers of our soul. "My God, I love you," this word can include the holiest act of man in itself, the greatest of man: the mystery of his love for the infinite God.

One more thing must be expressed about this love for God so that it won't be misunderstood. The flame of the impulse to forget oneself, to devote oneself to the higher, burns always somewhere on the altar of the heart of every human being (even if it's as an avenging fire of the lost who no longer can love). But this flame is not yet love for God by itself, not even when it rises up to that one that it calls its God. Such an impulse upwards only becomes Christian love when God redeems it in his grace.

However, that means two things: God must preserve this highest of man (always preserve it anew, save him from it again and again) from becoming the highest expression of man's pride, of presumption of his God-equality by his own power, of flaming impatience that wants to conquer God on its own and pull him down to itself. Only when the inaccessible majesty and unapproachable holiness of eternal God humbles man; when he adoringly falls down freely before the distant God for his redemption from himself and even suppresses his desire to be near to God; when he is ready for any of God's decrees, asking whether

God wants man to come near him, only then does the flame of his desire for God burn purely. However, man is only capable of this through the grace of him who was the Son in the innermost sanctuary of the Father and nevertheless served the Lord as servant on the damned fields of this earth, silently and obediently. And further: Even the *pure* flame upwards would not yet be *the* love that God wants from us because he has presented it to us. Even the purest desire of man for the infinite God on its own would only circle around the Unapproachable from a distance. That we can do more, that we come before his countenance, that we can succeed in viewing him—the content of eternal life—as he is and partake of his innermost love, that is the act of *his* love, that is only possible because he himself in the Holy Spirit has poured out his ultimate, absolute love into our hearts—into hearts that were only impotence, sin, and emptiness. That is only possible because he has come to us, because the incomprehensibility of his love has taken place which has loved itself into where nothing was that was worthy of such love or could provoke it. We do not ascend up to him, rather he descended down to us. Because he found us, we can seek him with our love, and this is nothing other than the—almost frightened—concession of his love, which itself takes us to the heart of God. The highest act of which we are capable is demanded of us—what else can we call it than love? But it would remain as distant from him as everything else if his love would not mysteriously transform it into what is truly love that fills the eternities of God and redeemed man. Therefore we only love him when we don't forget that our love is his love which became ours at the time when the spear of hating man penetrated the heart of God so that it spilled out into the God-empty world. Therefore the prayer of our love can only be: "You love me," and the trembling petition, "Grant that I may let myself be loved by you. For even this is once more your gift."

But does this love live in us? Certainly love can, as strongly as death, glow in a human being almost without his noticing it. The ultimate in man doesn't have to be the purest, and there are people who do great things quietly. But nevertheless we all know that our love for God is poor and weak, that perhaps we want to love him with good will. However, we can't say that his love fills our entire heart, entire soul, mind, and all our strength. But we

have to love God more and more lest the great disappointment
of a worthless life comes over us, lest one day we have to cry that
we have gone through this time and have not loved, have to cry
like a child that notices at its mother's grave how much the silent
heart down below had deserved to be loved. But love is really a
peculiar thing. One says that one cannot order it up, and it seems
almost as if even our own good will is much too superficial to be
able to penetrate into those depths of the soul and open them in
which the hidden waters of love rise or sink according to their
own law. However, one thing is certain, whoever wants to honestly love God already loves him. He wouldn't be able to if God's
grace had not already touched man's heart and already taken
possession of love's final desire. We can at least let love grow, can
help remove the hindrances so that it is able to penetrate all of
man more and more. We can pray for it so that he himself, who
is the object of our love, visits us with the sweet omnipotence of
his grace, breaks open the wells of the deep, and quenches the
arid land of our soul with his love.

If it often seems to us that we have no power over our cold
heart, we still are able to do one thing: pay attention to the silent,
shy, almost unconscious stirring of this love of God, to the quiet
calls for God by our restless heart. The thousand affairs of our
life make us tired and morose; even our joys become stale. We
sense how even our friends are still distant from us, how even the
words of love from our most intimate friends ring to the ear of
our soul only as from afar, dimly and coolly. Everything that the
world acclaims we feel more and more as empty bustling without
true value. The new becomes old, the days pass by, mere knowledge is cold and empty, life goes along, wealth escapes us, popu-
larity is just a whim, senses age, the world is in flux, friends die.
And all that is the lot of normal life, is what people don't quite
count as suffering and pain. In addition is all the pain and bitterness that can fill a human being, all the tears, all the necessities of body and soul. But it is grace when this realization of the
finiteness and transitoriness of all things really seizes man. People
avoid this realization. If a material possession didn't still the
heart's yearning, then one hopes that the next will. However,
whoever pays attention to this realization, to this unrest and
this unstilled desire of the soul, whoever understands what this

seemingly so unfortunate disposition means in discovering limits and ends everywhere, he creates space in his heart for the love of God. He sees that only one can captivate his whole heart with all its thinking and feeling, that only one alone is constant, one alone faithful, one alone can be everything for us, one alone can possess us entirely. And when we feel this disappointment in the world, which every Christian must feel, that only one is qualified to accept our entire nature which we want to give away in the overpowering urge to love, if we endure this disappointment without despairing and without deceiving ourselves, then we begin to love God. We crave something but don't know what. But we are certain that it is something that the world cannot give. And we must only give this unknown, desired, and beloved being its true name: God. Then the love of God wakes in our soul almost automatically. Man craves almost automatically the God of his heart and his share of eternity. He begins almost automatically to seek him who alone still remains when everything else collapses, the only one who always surrounds him and loves him, the God of the longing of our poor heart. Another time it is not the disappointment in this little world that awakens the love of God in us but, rather thankfully, silent joy. We encounter a good human being, someone did something good to us, we are freed from burdensome fear or from harsh suffering, or otherwise a great, silent joy has entered into us. Almost automatically we sense how another, greater one is in charge behind this event, how this shimmer of joy is only a reflection of an eternal light. We feel thankfully how quietly God moved closely past us and blessed us. Then we are filled almost automatically with new, living knowledge that he is good and great and full of mercy. His nearness clutches us, and his blessing awakens love in us.

When God visits us with suffering or joy, when his love wakes in our soul, then we must join in this urging from the bottom of our soul. We must not drown out God's voice in us with new noise of the world, with diversion and other activity, the voice that speaks to us of his love out of its quiet longing for God. Everything in us should join in the subdued praying of our restless heart: "Oh God, you near, great one, you, my God, you alone are good, I love you."

What we have done so that the love for God stirs in us, what then stirs in us, is small and insignificant. Still insignificant because it must prove itself in the hard reality of the everyday, in faithfulness, obedience, and love of our neighbor. Small because it is only love for God because God himself transforms it through his Holy Spirit into the love which alone finds God's heart. But may we therefore ignore what we have to do ourselves, what comes as his grace in the form of our work, our prayer of love, if it wants to become the true love for God?

This mysterious rising of the waters of love from the hidden depths of our being, this tendency of the soul toward its God in which we only have to join in, would be much greater and more irresistible if we ourselves would not rubble over these springs through sin, if we would have a purer heart. What our Lord said has always been part of the most indisputable experience of religious life: "Blessed are the pure of heart, for they shall see God."[1] Only good people or at least people who have an honest, active desire for goodness can love God who is goodness itself. Even when grievous guilt doesn't burden the soul and hasn't extinguished love, how much other sins and all evil habits hinder the uplifting of love! People who just want to fulfill their most necessary Christian duties, who consider all conscientiousness and care beyond that as eccentricity, who only enter before God's countenance in prayer and reception of the sacraments with inner aversion, people for whom all spiritual life is an unpleasant obligation which one quickly attends to in order to turn to more enjoyable things, people who, satisfied with themselves, arrange their duty according to what they want to do—such people will never be able to love God with their whole heart. Their heart is dulled to God's courting for their love. Whoever loves God encounters his God every time. However, whoever is not prepared to renounce everything sinful is afraid to encounter God. He could demand something from him that a human being doesn't want to give. However, the more we follow the voice of our conscience, the more seriously, decisively, and perseveringly we do that which we immediately recognize as our obligation, the more

1. Translator's note: Matt 5:8.

we can penetrate into the next world, the nearer we come to God. The perception of his holy goodness grows, a holy relationship arises more and more between the pure soul and holy God, and we begin to love God with our whole soul, with our whole heart, with our whole mind, and with all our strength.

If we want to grow in love, we must not only pay attention to our quiet stirrings, we must not only prepare a pure heart for it, we must also pray *for* it. It is God who effects beginning, growth, and perfection of holy love in us according to his pleasure. He loved us first, it was his grace which spoke to us in the first stirrings of love which alone can purify our heart. Thus he wants us to pray for this grace: "Increase, Oh God, your love in us!" If we have to fear the passion of our heart, if our spirit wants to become insensitive to the love of God, if we ask ourselves anxiously whether we love the darkness more than the light, more than God, then we want to beg for his mercy, ask him that he let his love grow in us and make us firm. Oh Jesus, let us always fear and love your holy name because you never take away your guidance from those whom you found in the firmness of your love. A greater grace than the love of God has never been granted to any human being. It comprises our true life, it is our happiness, the peace of our restless heart, the content of our eternity. Shouldn't we pray for this love? Won't the Father hear us when we request nothing else from him than that he take us to his heart, when we desire no other wealth than his love?

This is how we want to pray: "Let me love you, my God. What do I have in heaven, what on earth other than you, you, God of my heart and my share in eternity? Let me cling to you. Beloved Lord, be the center of my heart, purify it so that it loves you. Let my happiness be your blessedness, your beauty, your goodness and holiness. Be always with me, and when I am tempted to leave you, my God, do not let me. Leave me only one thing: Your love. Let it grow in me; your love is the highest thing and let it never cease, and without it I am nothing. Let me be united with you one day eternally through love."

4

Prayer in the Everyday

Prayer is exalted. It is a word out of the depths of the heart. And what is more exalted than the simple, believing, and loving heart? It is a word spoken to God in such a way that he listens to it lovingly and takes it to his heart. And what can be of more moving exaltedness than this loving listening by the Eternal to the stammering word of his child? Prayer is a prayer in the Holy Spirit. What can be of more astonishing exaltedness than the voice of the Spirit which makes the eternities quake and fills the abysses of God when it carries the intimidated word of the small creature on its wings before the throne of God so that the earth's weeping is heard in the innermost chambers of that eternity which God built for the exultation of his own life? Prayer is exalted. And whoever has grasped that becomes frightened when he wants to begin to pray.

Then can such an action be the business of the everyday? Of the everyday with its monotony of constant sameness, of the everyday with its everyday gray mood, with the dullness of hearts that are tired and discouraged?

But there must be a prayer of the everyday. For it is written: "One should always pray and not give up" (Luke 18:1). And again: "Be alert and always keep on praying" (Eph 6:18). And then: "Pray without ceasing" (1 Thess 5:17); "rejoice in hope, endure in affliction, persevere in prayer" (Rom 12:12).

We want to say two things about prayer of the everyday. They can be comprised in two exhortations: Pray in the everyday; pray the everyday.

Pray in the everyday. With prayer in the everyday, we mean that regular prayer which is practiced without regard to the desire and mood of the moment, prayer that man demands of himself as his own duty and cherished custom without being actually bound to do it; prayer that is familiar with specific times for prayer, that is connected to particular times of the day and opportunities, with the morning and evening, with mealtimes. Prayer of the everyday is prayer at the ringing of the Angelus, the Rosary by oneself or with one's family, the silent private visit to a church and the tabernacle outside of the times of common divine service, and other devout practices of old customs as, for example, showing respect while passing a church or an image of the cross, making the Sign of the Cross while slicing a loaf of bread, the Sign of the Cross which a child requests and receives from its parents in the evening—these and many similar things are brief petitions for blessing and thus prayer of the everyday.

Such prayer is difficult in the everyday. It becomes difficult for many not to forget this prayer in the everyday. How much of this custom of prayer in large cities is no longer practiced and is forgotten! And how much of what the city-dweller, if he is still Christian, theoretically still acknowledges as duty or Christian custom has only a very meager existence in practice which is threatened by being totally forgotten. One's spirit and heart are filled with other things. One supposedly doesn't have time. At least not for such—as it appears—bothersome and somewhat old-fashioned things that appear to resemble other submerged things from childhood. They have never officially been done away with, they just manage to exist, but they are so little a creative force in real life that one could easily admit that nothing would be changed in real life if these remnants from the old days of one's parents and one's own childhood were to totally disappear. Such prayer in the everyday is difficult. It's difficult not to forget it entirely in the everyday because it doesn't have any footing on which to flourish in these times and environment and seldom finds a heart for its fresh blooming that is untroubled by its unbelieving environment and that is able to grant the strength from its own innermost solidarity with God for strong growth of prayer in the everyday.

If it's difficult not to let prayer in the everyday disappear slowly and unnoticed, then it's even more difficult to really "pray" prayer in the everyday and not just perform it. Oh, how much of our everyday prayer is really "prayed," and what is only mouthed? How often are heart and mind far from everything we pray, how often does the word to God, from heart to heart, become the recital of a formula during which one is only concerned that it is done, during which, however, one is no longer with him to whom one says the prayer! The everyday routinizes prayer in the everyday.[1] It becomes exterior, mechanical, heartless, lip-prayer and consummation of an external action that one carries out as quickly as possible in order to apply oneself once more to more enjoyable things. This prayer becomes, as it were, a time grudgingly granted to God because one can't very well do otherwise and, in any case, doesn't want to spoil things with him. And then all too easily the so everyday but also shocking thing can happen: that one prays, but one's heart is far from God, that one pays lip-service to God, but one's heart doesn't go along; but nevertheless one imagines to have fulfilled one's obligation to God. As if there could be any other satisfaction of obligation before the Searcher of the heart than that this external action is filled and fulfilled with the pure disposition of the heart.

It can also be that inner man is suffering from the stress of what his prayer is and what it is supposed to be. He is suffering because his heart doesn't go along with the august words of worship, praise, thanks, petition, awe and repentance, and similar sentiments of which we speak in prayer. He is suffering because he wants to pray—often and daily—but apparently cannot pray. An inner paralysis has overcome his heart, and he has the impression that his honesty forbids him from dissembling what he in truth cannot do, and his loyalty to himself and to God prescribes that he wait until the wells of the depths of his heart with their waters of grace, of spontaneous experience and deep emotion, automatically start anew and thus enable prayer that really is genuine outpouring of the heart. This difficulty may also lead serious and thoughtful people to pray infrequently. People who

---

1. Translator's note: *Der Alltag veralltäglicht das Gebet im Alltag.*

seldom pray, whose everyday is prayerless, not because they have succumbed to the superficial bustle of the everyday but because they are interior and forthright and only want to do in prayer what really comes from the interior, who are not of the opinion that one only has to will it and prayer would become a genuine word of inner man from the depths of his heart.

But nevertheless despite all these difficulties, the old Christian maxim and way of life remain correct and true for us also: to pray daily, to pray in the everyday, not to limit prayer to the infrequent lofty hours of inner emotion and astonishment in which man begins to pray, as it were, automatically because he is faithful and has not lost sight of God entirely. We must comprehend the necessity of everyday prayer. For this everyday prayer is the prerequisite and consequence of the great and noble hours of prayer.

Certainly all prayer is not equal. Certainly there are prayers in fleeting and infrequent moments in which the angel of God touches our heart so that it burns with awe before the majesty of the present God, with homesickness and hope for the peace of the Lord, with repentance which transforms an entire life, with love for eternal Love. Certainly we like to value *these* moments more highly than everyday prayer and tend to call them alone prayer. But such moments of reprieve are infrequent. And what use would they be for us if they really didn't move our entire life and breathe their spirit into it? What use would they be to us if they became more and more infrequent, weaker and weaker like the ideas of a wasted genius whose inspirations become more and more rare? However, how else are these two dangers of remaining ineffective and waning away to be remedied than through *daily* prayer? Only when we pray daily do we create the prerequisites for the great hours of prayer. Only when we exert ourselves, even when it is burdensome, to keep our heart open, keep our spirit alert, our attention and readiness keen, only then the great hours of prayer won't be forgone, the hours in which God suddenly encounters us anew and unexpectedly calls out a crucial cue to us that will affect a large piece of our life (What if we failed to hear it and weren't ready for it?). Or—in an hour of great trial, of radical temptation, of amazing happiness or annihilating need, in an hour of extreme loneliness and piercing pain, and in other great days and nights of life—he demands an answer (which is prayer) that is decisive for now and eternity. How should we have this openness of the heart, this alertness of the spirit and this readiness in these fateful hours of life unless we had previously obeyed the word to be on watch and pray, if we hadn't prayed in the everyday? If we don't pray daily, that means look for God daily, listen for God's word daily (even when a call from above doesn't come right away), prepare ourselves daily for the critical trials of our life, then there would be the danger that we slowly become blind and deaf, indifferent and slothful. And then will we even notice the critical intersections on our road of life, will a sudden storm find us standing firm, will we possess the capability for moral decisions, if we haven't previously remained on watch in our everyday prayer? And if we don't survive these fateful hours of life (when life and death are at issue), the hours which quietly and without forewarning and without much ado assail man, can we say that we are innocent, we didn't mean it that way, we had been taken by surprise, we hadn't judged the situation correctly and didn't foresee the consequences? Can we say that when earlier, slothful and dull, we didn't want to remain awake through daily prayer? In the intellectual and spiritual realm also, there is something like procedural practice and scrutiny which alone make it possible to survive the crisis.

And when God's hour and fervent, great prayer is over, how will it become more than an unfruitful festivity in our life, how will it be converted into the slow, patient work on inner man, into work which changes and transforms the somber life, the ordinariness of the everyday into indefatigable striving for that image that was shown to us for an instant in the lofty moments of charismatic prayer? How can this decisive event take place other than through prayer in the everyday, that—together with God's angel of grace—under the burden and exertion of the everyday, wrestles with this gray workaday morning and that fretful evening exhaustion so that at least a weak glimmer of the light of eternity shines over it? Only when this fire of the Spirit that descended upon us in a happy hour divides itself into little flames of fire and lights up the everyday hours so that we can pray as well as possible. Then the fiery Spirit will really grasp our life that, for the most part, is threaded together with small, gray moments. Everyday prayer is the prerequisite and consequence of the great hours of grace in Christian life. And therefore it is vital and indispensable.

But also a further, weightier thing tells us to pray in the everyday: The glory of God. The Lord is not only our God on the holy days of life. He didn't create the exalted so that he could have it back for his glory. He also willed into existence the petty, the insignificant, the ever-the-same which fills our life. We are his servants not only when we fill his mighty cathedrals or when his mysteries are effected in us in mysterious splendor and beauty. We are his servants and handmaids also in the field and in the workshop, at table and in the bedroom, behind a desk and in front of a laundry tub. All this is also for his glory and the praise of his name. Must it not be that we remember in the everyday that we and our everydayness belong to him and live for his glory so that his praise must rise up from this life, so that we must say: "In God's name," that we must constantly say a good word of blessing over this everyday, that we must always pray in the everyday?

Oh everyday prayer! You are poor and a little tattered and the worse for wear like the everyday itself. August thoughts and exalted feelings are difficult for you. You are not an exalted symphony in a great cathedral, but more like a devout song, well-intended and coming from the heart, a little monotonous and naive. But, prayer of the everyday, you are the prayer of loyalty and reliability, the prayer of selfless, unrewarded service to the divine majesty, you are the dedication which makes the gray hours light and the trivial moments great. You don't ask about the experience of the one praying, but about the honor of God. You don't want to experience something, but to believe. Your gait may sometimes be weary, but you still walk. Sometimes you may appear to come just from the lips and not from the heart. But isn't it better that at least the lips are blessing God than when the entire human being becomes mute? And isn't there more hope then that the sound from the lips will find an echo in the heart than when everything in man remains mute? And in our prayer-poor times, what one chides oneself or others for as lip-prayer is most often in reality the prayer of a poor but loyal heart that laboriously and honestly, in spite of all the weakness, weariness, and inner discontent, is at least continuing to dig a small shaft through which a small ray of the eternal light falls into our heart that is buried by the everyday.

Pray in the everyday! Rouse yourself constantly from weariness and indifference! Pray personally! Try to make a personal prayer out of everyday prayer so that you escape from the hustle and bustle around you and in you to find you yourself; from excited haste into serenity, from the narrowness of the world into the breadth of faith, and away from you to God, and not just to the prayer formula that you once learned as a child!

Pray regularly! Demand from yourself what you have set for yourself as your obligation in prayer! Be lord over your emotions and moods! Pray regularly!

Learn to pray! It is a grace. But it is also a matter of good will, an art which has to be practiced and tested. One can learn to collect oneself before prayer, to become quiet inside and to reflect on what one wants to do: to lift one's heart up to God. One can learn to speak without a formula to God about one's need, about one's life, even about one's secret reluctance to have anything to do with him, to speak with him about one's obligations, to speak about one's loved ones, about one's own feelings, about the world and its need, about the dearly departed, to speak with him about himself: that he is so great and so distant, so incomprehensible but so splendid, that he is the truth and we are the lie, he is love and we are selfishness, he is life and we are death, he is fulfillment and we are longing. One can learn to bestow a relaxed composure to one's body, to become inwardly at rest, to bring impudent everyday thoughts and everyday moods to rest, so that one is finally able to perceive one's own soul, the soul that is shy and has few but essential words and a song that one can only sing to God. One can learn to make a prayer out of reading sacred Scripture. One can learn during evening prayer to give the day's experiences the right sense and the true direction toward God, to let the day enter in the right form into those deeper spaces of the soul in which the temporal is stored. In the right form, that is, without bitterness and hate, in kindness and serenity, in confident repentance, in sincerity and dedication to God. In the everyday one can learn to hallow through prayer dead moments in which one can do nothing, in which one must wait and stand around. One can learn to be reminded of God by the vexations and the little joys of the day. Such and similar tactics of one who wants to pray in the everyday can be learned and practiced. You can learn them too! Pray in the everyday!

Pray the everyday! There is yet a higher ideal of consecrating the everyday through prayer. Happy is he who always prays at certain intervals in the everyday! He himself will certainly not become of the everyday. And certainly we shall always have to pray explicitly. But the suffering of spiritual man in the everyday is not quite surmounted by this. For even when we frequently pray *in* the everyday, the everyday itself always seems to remain what it is: everydayish. It is frequently interrupted for our salvation but not yet transformed. Our soul still seems to remain a road on which the convoy of this world rolls along endlessly with its countless bagatelles, with its idle talk and bother, its curiosity and its empty trivialities. Our soul still seems to be the marketplace on which hawkers come from every direction to gather and sell the miserable riches of this world, where in everlasting, deadening unrest, we ourselves, men and the world, spread out their trifles. Our soul in the everyday only seems to be a huge barn into which everything from everywhere is unloaded haphazardly day after day until it is filled to the roof with the everyday. And so it seems to go along for an entire lifetime in the everyday until—yes, until that hour which we call our death—all the junk which was our life is removed from the barn. But what will we ourselves be and remain who for a lifetime were only everyday, thus bustle and wasteland filled with gossip and commotion? What will result from our life when the massive burden of death relentlessly presses the true contents out of our hollow life, out of the many days and long years that have remained empty? Will more remain than those few moments into which the grace of love or of honest prayer to God slipped in shyly as into a corner of our life filled with everyday rubbish?

But how should we turn this need of the everyday around? How do we, in midst of this everydayness, find our way to the only necessary one who only is God? How can the everyday itself become a song of praise to God, that is, prayer? One thing is clear from the first. We are not able to pray explicitly all the time, we can't flee the everyday, we would take it along with us no matter where we went because we ourselves are our everyday:

our daily heart, our lackluster spirit, and the trivial love that also makes the great meager and ordinary. And therefore the route can only go right through the middle of the everyday, its need, and its obligation. Therefore the everyday cannot be overcome through flight but only by steadfastness and by a transformation. Therefore God must be sought and found *in* the world, therefore the everyday must become God's day, going out into the world must become going inward with God, the everyday must become a "day of recollection." The everyday itself must be prayed.

But how is that supposed to happen? How will the everyday itself become prayer? Through selflessness and prayer. Oh, if we were willing and intelligent disciples, we couldn't have a better master than the everyday for inner and spiritual man! The same long hours, the monotony of obligations, the work that everyone finds matter-of-fact, the long and bitter effort for which no one is thankful, the exhaustion and sacrifice of old age, the disappointments and failures, the misunderstandings and lack of understanding, the unfulfilled aspirations, the small humiliations, the unavoidable dogmatism of adults toward youth, the likewise unavoidable heartlessness of youth toward adults, the minor complaints of the body, the unfriendliness of the weather, the frictions of closely living together, such and a thousand other things that fill the everyday, how can they, how could they make man serene and selfless?

If he were to comply with this so human but so divine pedagogy, if he said yes, if he didn't fight against it, if he took the everyday upon himself as self-evident, without complaint and without commotion, as that which is obviously his due! And if man would let his egoticity[2] be destroyed by the everyday, slowly but surely—oh, the guidance of God in the everyday is of uncanny accuracy—then the love for God would awake by itself in our heart, a still and chaste love. For what hinders man from loving God? Only he himself stands in the way and in the light. In the everyday, however, one can slowly die to oneself each day, without commotion and without rhetoric. No one will notice.

---

2. Translator's note: *Ichhaftigkeit*, which could be translated as "I-ishness."

Not even oneself. But continuously one wall after another will be knocked down by the fortunes of the everyday, walls that the anxious I had built for its defense. And when this I stops building walls, and says yes to insecurity, and suddenly—almost with happy astonishment—notices that one doesn't need these defensive walls, that one doesn't (as one thought up to now) need to be unhappy when life takes this or that joy away that one held for indispensable, that one doesn't have to despair when this or that success fails to occur or this or that plan founders, when one notices through this education of the everyday that one becomes rich through giving, fulfilled through renunciation, joyous through sacrifice, loved through love of the other, then man will become selfless and thereby free. If free, then capable of the great, spacious love of the free, limitless God. Everything depends on *how* we bear the everyday. It can make us everyday. However, it can also make us free from ourselves as nothing else can. However, if we accomplished this freedom and selflessness, then this love, which arises by itself, would soar through all things, directly through the heart of things, would soar out into the infinite expanses of God in longing and holy desire and also take along all the lost things of the everyday as a song of praise of the divine Splendor. Our cross of the everyday—on which alone our self-seeking can completely die because it has to be crucified inconspicuously if it is supposed to die—would become the rising of our love because it would arise from the grave of our own I. And if everything in the everyday becomes such dying, everything in the everyday becomes the rising of love. Then the entire everyday becomes the breathing of love, breathing of longing, of loyalty, of faith, of readiness, of devotion to God; the everyday really becomes itself, wordless prayer! It will remain what it was: difficult, without rhetoric, everyday, inconspicuous. It must be so. Only in this way does it serve the love of God, for only so does it take us away from ourselves. But if we let ourselves be taken by the everyday, our longing, our self-assertion, our obstinacy, our walled-in ourselfness, that is, if we don't become bitter in our bitterness, ordinary in our ordinariness, everyday in our everydayness, disappointed in our disappointment, if we let ourselves be educated through the everyday to kindness, to patience, to peace and understanding, to forbearance and meekness, to forgiveness and endurance, to selfless loyalty, then the everyday is no longer the everyday, then it is prayer. Then all diversity becomes one in the love of God, all effusion remains collected in God, all exteriority remains in God inwardly. Then all going out into the world, the everyday, becomes a going into God's unity, which is eternal life.

Pray the everyday! Beg for this noble art of Christian life which is so difficult because it is so easy!

Prayer in the everyday, prayer of the everyday! If our everyday is an everyday accompanied by prayer and itself prayed, then these poor, passing days of our life, the days of ordinariness and banal bitterness, the days which always are equally indifferent and troublesome, would flow into the one day of God, into the great day which knows no evening. Let us pray for this day every day of our lives just as we learned as a child and as we practiced it! Then it can also be said of us: "I am confident of this, that the one who began a good work—good work of daily prayer—in you will continue to complete it until the day of Christ Jesus" (Phil 1:6).

5

The Prayer of Need

Accusations and charges sometimes can be justified. But once they have been raised, the defendant is always at a disadvantage—perhaps even unavoidably—because he has been accused, and often others perceive his defense and justification as a secret admission of guilt. If someone has to defend himself, then people think that something is wrong, otherwise this entire defense procedure would not be required.

Because this unusual law unfortunately really exists, one can comprehend that it is a difficult task to assume the defense of the prayer of petition,[1] to hear the charges calmly, to take them seriously, really seriously, what tormented and bitter people say against the prayer of petition, and still after all the charges and countercharges, after all the arguments and objections, to believe and inwardly to understand that we have to petition and may not let up.

That is difficult. For the plaintiff in this case is the entire course of human events. All the bitter and despondent hearts have appointed themselves as the judges. And the united nations of all the unhappy people are witnesses for the prosecution. And who does not feel unhappy if he can make an accusation? But even if one wanted to strictly select the prosecution's witnesses and wanted to reject the impudent and the grumblers and the fortune-hunters and the frivolous—in the end we are all poor

---

1. Translator's note: *Bittgebet*. Rahner uses the verb and the noun, *bitten* and *Bitte*, throughout this chapter. They are translated as "petition" or "beg" depending on the context.

and unhappy and are all gathered in the witness box against the prayer of petition. And all these people come from everywhere. They come from all countries, from all times, all ages and classes. And what they have to say against the prayer of petition is one and the same charge of despair, of disappointment, of angry or weary unbelief. And this charge is (oh, one could go on endlessly):

We prayed, and God did not answer. We cried, and he remained mute. We wept tears that consumed our hearts. We were not allowed before his countenance. We could have proven to him that our claims are modest, that they are realizable, since he is the Almighty. We could have demonstrated to him that fulfillment of these petitions is in the vital interest of his glory in the world and of his kingdom. How should anyone otherwise still be able to believe that he is the God of justice and the Father of mercy and the God of all consolation, that he exists at all? Beyond all claims and counterclaims, we wanted to appeal to his heart, to the heart that simply has mercy and liberally commands justice and other considerations to comply. We would have had faith that moves mountains (in case that were the only thing lacking). We would have shown him why we have every reason to despair because of his silence. We would have had endless material on file: the unanswered prayer for babies who starved to death, the unheard complaint for the little ones who suffocated from tonsillitis, the misery of violated young women, of children who were beaten to death, of the exploited labor slaves, of betrayed women, of those crushed by injustice, of the "liquidated," of the cripples, of those dishonored.

In addition to our exterior need, we would have shown him the inner torments which don't affect God, the torment which arises from the ancient questions, which have been waiting for answers since Adam's time. Why is the scoundrel successful and the just one the dunce, why does the same lightning fall on the good and sinners alike, why do the fathers sin and the children pay for it, why are lies so prevalent, why does injustice prosper so well, why is world history a single stream of stupidity, crudity, and brutality?

And after these questions we would have implored him: By your glory, by your splendor, by your name in this world which you ultimately have to account for, see to it that we can find your trail a little more clearly in this forlorn world. The traces of your wisdom, your justice and kindness. But please, we would have said further, we want to experience your help so that people can't say that this much help is unavoidable even if there is no God, so they couldn't say that everyone inevitably has that many winning numbers in this world's lifelong lottery game whether one prays in advance or doesn't, one doesn't have to ascribe the few chance winners to the power of God.

We would have appealed to his Son who knows how we feel emotionally and physically because he shared our life. We could do all that. We would have done all that, we actually did all of that. For we *have* prayed. We have *prayed*. We have begged. We have lifted ardent, entreating words to heaven. It didn't do any good. We cried like lost children who know that in the end the policeman will take them home. But no one came who wiped *our* tears away and consoled us. We have prayed. But we were not heard. We called. But no answer came. We screamed, but everything remained so mute that we would have seemed ridiculous to ourselves if it hadn't been extorted from us by need and despair.

This is how the prayer of petition is charged. But when one brings the charge, the demand for a case in court, then the prosecutors are not united. The majority draws this brutal conclusion from the charges: There is no purpose in praying. There is no God to hear a prayer of petition, he doesn't exist at all, or he dwells in such dreadful glory that the scream of need doesn't penetrate the ear of his heart; rather, he allows his creation to go the way of its bloody history for his own glory, untroubled by the agony of the world, just as the great ones of this earth wage atrocious wars and remain untouched only in order to enter into history because of their unique accomplishments.

However, every once in a while when it seems to be more comfortable in the world, when one finds it quite bearable down here (if it would only continue to be so fine and progressive!), then suddenly one has all kinds of very profound metaphysical considerations which would forbid God from interfering too concretely in the process of world history. Oh, it isn't fitting at all for our exalted God to meddle in the trifles of this world. In the very beginning he must have built the world's clock so that it runs quite exactly and correctly and, if possible, for an unfore-seeable time, without one having to notice anything of him in its running. The world must be so sublimely meaningful, so final and able to run its course by itself, that no one at all should be allowed to touch it. A prayer of petition to God is childish; one thinks of God too pettily and holds oneself for too important. This is how one reasons high-mindedly (one can afford it, it is going pretty well for one) and manages to get by without the prayer of petition (but not without wages, physicians, and the police). However, when one fares unbearably again, one is furious that one is not heard immediately (if possible, even before one has begun to ask) and therefore declares the prayer of petition to be superfluous for this reason.

The minority of the prosecuting counsels are of another opinion. They want to allow the prayer of petition. But only for requesting the noble goods of the soul. Praying for our daily bread is no longer allowed, nor for bodily health and a long life, nor against lightning and storms, for deliverance from pestilence, hunger, and need, nor from dismal, miserable times. Rather, just for purity of heart, for patience and willingness to suffer, for submission to God's will. The rest of the prayer of petition is only a childlike formulation of the willingness to submit unconditionally to God's inexorable will. One doesn't beg God to avoid evil things but for the strength to bear them. Prayer would only be heard—less a few miracles which one couldn't expect—in the interiority of the heart, not in the hard unequivocality of this world, which takes its inexorable course in nature and history in dispassionate objectivity also over hearts that are bleeding.

Those are the most important charges against the prayer of petition. According to the first, man remains on earth permanently alone and rejects the hope of help from heaven in this world. According to the second, man abandons the earth from the beginning without a struggle and flees to heaven.

Those are the charges against the prayer of petition. And naturally God himself is the accused. However, he remains silent. He calmly allows the accusations and charges. He remains silent. He remains obstinately silent. He remains silent through the millennia. He let it be said that he won't speak until he comes to judge. And therefore the charges against the prayer of petition can continue, the charges from broken hearts, the charges from racked minds, the charges with which cynics or upstart poets demonstrate their acumen or their secret godlessness.

But *we* do want to pray and beg. For we feel the torment and the trials of the complaints against the prayer of petition; however, the unconquerable power of faith lives in us which hopes against all hope and continues to pray against all apparent disappointment. For we have been given the mandate: This is how you are to pray: "Our Father . . . give us this day our daily bread." And we don't want to be found right by taking God to court;[2] rather, we want to find the ear of God's mercy. We don't want to solve the mysteries of life to which the prayer of petition also belongs but to learn the prayer of petition. We don't want to be more astute than the charge against the prayer of petition. For we don't want to examine the rope from which we hang over the abyss of the nothing but to cling to it so that we don't fall into the abyss of despair. We only want enough light and strength so that we can continue to pray, so that our heart doesn't despair and our mouth begin to curse, we want to continue to pray until . . . until God speaks and his word becomes the word of mercy and eternal consolation.

What do we want to say to this charge against the prayer of petition? If we try for a moment to silence our lust for life and our hunger for happiness (or are they really the one and the ultimate things of the world that always have to have the last word?), then the voice of God tells us in our conscience a few very essential things about these charges against the prayer of petition:

It asks us: Why do you suddenly demand relief from God for what you have brought upon yourselves? Aren't you responsible because you have sinned? Aren't you only screaming because now *you* are faring poorly, while you remain placidly silent when misfortune and crudity pursue other people? Don't you only want to be involved with God when you can't manage it alone, but otherwise you want him as far away as possible, you red-faced hypocrites, because you are happiest when you can forget him for a while? Aren't you quite satisfied with the course of the world as long as it favors you? But then you think that God's

---

2. Translator's note: In idiomatic use *ins Gericht gehen mit* can also mean to "take someone to task."

kingdom[3] in the world is in danger when the rate of the Reich bonds, which *you* bought, is falling? (Just as princes usually start to become quite devout when their thrones begin to totter.) Have you comprehended yet that God's glory in the world is the cross of his Son? You claim to believe in eternal happiness in the other world! Why are you so enamored of this world like those who only know the meager luxury of this earth? Aren't you the kind of people for whom a bird in the hand is better than two in the bush? And isn't this "rational" position just the opposite of Christianity? Don't you self-satisfied and supercilious people see God's blessing and his sanction of your endeavors in your own prosperity, but then don't you ask indignantly about what you had not done correctly when he denies success to the ruses of your self-seeking? Aren't you full of childish impatience when you can't wait for the day when he, the Eternal and Patient, will reckon with all of world history, and he won't come too late anywhere to straighten out all the confused and mistaken things of time in the expanses of his eternity? Have you actually comprehended who God is and who you are? Comprehended that God's ways and God's judgments, if he is different as God, must be such that you do *not* comprehend them?[4] Comprehended that the creature *can* never take God to court?[5] Comprehended that you are not able to comprehend his love and mercy, precisely these things, and that they must appear to you as wrath and justice? And again: Haven't *you* sinned and brought about the disaster? Why do you want the cause but demand that the effect be given to you as a gift also? Can any one of you say that you have not deserved "that"? If anyone says that, then he is a liar, and the truth is not in him.[6] Because man is a sinner, and every sin deserves more than it suffers. And again: Have you ever taken sin seriously? You liars have thousands of excuses. It's caused by heredity and environment, or it is not meant to be that evil, for

---

3. Translator's note: The German word for the "kingdom" of God is *Reich*, which is otherwise usually translated as "empire." Cf. also the use of "the Third *Reich*" in the text.

4. Translator's note: Cf. Isa 55:7ff.

5. Translator's note: This is the same phrase explained in footnote 2.

6. Translator's note: Cf. 1 John 2:4 and John 8:44.

in the end one doesn't have anything against our dear God, but he must understand too that one wants to have a little bit of happiness in this valley of tears. Even if one has to pick it from the forbidden tree, then it's regretful, but it's not our fault that there are so few unforbidden trees. That's how you try to turn sin into something else. But nevertheless it is sacrilege against the All-Holy, and it is nevertheless your work. Then why don't you bagatellize your need for once? For is it so bad that a good part of the species man regularly perishes in the struggle for existence? During the last few decades you were very much in favor of such theories! At any rate, the practice of such theories caused few sleepless nights for most of you.

Is it so self-evident that even I must find it quite normal? Why do you take yourselves for so important when you hold God's glory and God's will for so unimportant? Have you comprehended who I am and who you are when you begin to be evil and harsh, when the cry of your need doesn't immediately find the echo which your self-seeking and your obduracy expect?

Does God have to prove that he is good and holy, or rather, don't you have to prove that you love without reward and without life insurance? How do you know that all the stars have been extinguished when, in your opinion, it's getting dark around you? How do you know that you are falling into the abyss when you no longer know what you're supposed to hold on to? How do you know that he doesn't exist when you no longer are able to perceive and comprehend him? "Oh man, who are you, to argue with God?" (Rom 9:20).

And further: What about the "evils" from which you want to be saved? Are you sure that they are really evils when measured by the ultimate, by *my* standards? They may be, and it's just for this reason that I want you to petition. But are you able to make the final judgment about this, or do you have to leave that to me? Aren't you saying (when one listens precisely to the true sense of your petitions, which you won't even really admit to yourselves) in your prayer of petition: "Give me bread, give me health, security, and peace, oh, *then* I'll want to serve you, then I'll want to love you, inwardly and faithfully!" But did you do that when you had bread and an easy life? Or weren't bread and life themselves an "evil" for you because they seduced you to forget me, an evil from which my strong kindness had to redeem you so that you can find your salvation? No, if you really brought your true or supposed needs and evils before my countenance in prayer, you have come really to me, the Holy and Eternal, and you aren't just carrying on a monologue of blind egotism with yourselves in your prayer. You will recognize that if your petition is transformed into a question to me, into a question to my inscrutable wisdom and eternal goodness: What is better for me, need or happiness, success or failure, life or death? If your petition isn't transformed into this question in that moment when it penetrates into the silent incomprehensibility of my eternal designs, then this is a sign that you didn't pray but rebelled against the majesty of your God to whom worship is due just when you beg him for help in the need of your human existence.

This is how our conscience could answer the charges against the prayer of petition. But we haven't yet even named the essential answer that God gave to man. The answer which he gives by him himself becoming a beggar in this world, by his becoming flesh and letting the cry of need rise from his own tormented heart into the disconsolate silence of our distant God. When the lamenting and weeping choir of world history's prayer of petition threatened to suffocate and to become mute in despair because this lamenting choir had already lasted too long and still no other answer came than the endless promises of the Day of Judgment. Then the eternal God didn't order us with harsh words to continue praying until it pleased him to hear us in the coming of his eternal kingdom, rather he let his eternal Word become flesh to weep together with this lamenting choir: Lord, let your kingdom come, the kingdom in which all dreams are ended and you hear the weeping of the poor and the cry of need of all human agony.

The eternal Word of divine jubilation became the cry of human need in time and dwelt among us. That is our answer to the charges against the prayer of petition. This answer is called Jesus Christ. He doesn't teach us a metaphysics of the prayer of petition. He doesn't solve theoretically the dark issues of how the will for what is requested and the submission to God's will, of how the insusceptible freedom of God and the power of prayer over God's heart, of how the promise of hearing every prayer of petition in the name of Jesus and life's experience of unheard petitions, are all reconciled. However, he prays the prayer of petition for us. And therefore he is the answer to the charges against the prayer of petition as long as the God of eternity remains silent in this time of faith and he is not yet justified by the advent of the eternal kingdom of his justice and mercy. Our answer is Jesus Christ. He of whom it is written: "In the days when he was in the flesh, he offered prayers and supplications with loud cries and tears to the one who was able to save him from death, and he was heard because of his reverence" (Heb 5:7).

If Jesus Christ is the answer to our question, then his prayer of petition is our doctrine. Three words of his prayer of petition are meant: the word of realistic petition, the word of heavenly confidence, the word of unconditional submission. Jesus speaks the word of realistic petition: "Let this cup pass from me."[7] He prays it with the entire fervor of a human being hounded by anxiety and dread. He begs during the bloody sweat of anguish; he implores during the gasping torment of death. He doesn't petition for the exalted, sublime. He asks for the most wretched but most delightful thing for us mortals: for his life, for the passing over of the agony and ignominy of execution. His prayer of petition is of heavenly confidence: "I know that you always hear me" (John 11:42). His prayer of petition is a prayer of unconditional submission: "Not my will, but yours be done" is so completely unconditional submission that the God-forsaken, the failed one, the martyred one, while in agony on the cross devotedly and trustingly lays his soul into the hands of God.

How do these words form harmony in his soul? Jesus wrestles with the will of God until he bleeds but is always totally devoted to him. He shouts his need to heaven and is always certain of being heard. He knows that he will be heard always and in everything and wants to do nothing but the incomprehensible will of God. He really prays for his life with bloody fervor, and his prayer for his life is only an offer of his life for death. How mysterious is this unity of the most contradictory in Jesus' prayer of petition! Who can thoroughly interpret this mystery? But the mystery of the true Christian prayer of petition, of the God-man

---

7. Translator's note: Matt 26:39 and Mark 14:36.

prayer of petition, of the true prayer of petition of *every* Christian, is contained in this mystery in which, if we may be allowed to say it, as in Christ himself, the most godly and the most human are united and permeate each other while being unadulterated and unseparated. Truly Christian prayer of petition is totally human. The anxiety of earthly need, the demand for earthly preservation, the torment and the desire of the creature, rise and call to God initially not for himself but for his help for earthly bread for his hungry body, and for earthly life before death. Thus it is a cry of the most vital self-assertion, of the most immediate urge of life, a completely primitive, human cry of need. And yet more, this prayer of petition is quite godly. In midst of this defense of the earth before and, in a certain sense, against God, everything is given over to him, the Incomprehensible. Such an urge for life and such self-assertion let themselves willingly and from all sides and unconditionally be encompassed by God's will from which there is no appeal to a higher court. This urge for life doesn't want bread and life, rather the will of God even if it is hunger and death. And this prayer of petition is godly and human at the same time. Its human power and hope are enkindled by calling the Almighty who can do everything; by making an appeal to the Promise of God itself. And thus the prayer of petition becomes all the more full of blood, stronger and more human, precisely because it approaches *God*. And nevertheless: Because the prayer of petition lifts earthly need and earthly craving, earthly self-defense, into the light and the love of God in the interim, before the Essential, before God apparently for something higher, these things are pulled into that movement that carries everything, whether earthly fulfillment, or earthly need and downfall, into the life of God.

In this God-human, mysterious unity of the human will before God and submission to the will of God, in this unity in which God takes the will of the earth, devours it in his will and thus preserves it, the infallibility of the divine promise of hearing the true prayer of petition becomes possible and comprehensible. The Father's hearing belongs to the Son. It is promised to us as children of the Father and brothers of Christ. We are both, however, only to the extent that we have entered into the will of God. We must want God, his love, his glory. Everything egoistic in this will must be consumed by fire. Only then are we perfect children of God, then our prayer of petition is God-human, only then can we say together with the Son: "I know that you always hear me." Only then has the I that wants to be heard entered altogether into the Thou that hears, only then will that mysterious sympathy and pure, free harmony between God and man be completed through which man himself is truly able to want, strive for, and petition on his own. But at the same time what is wanted, strived for, asked for, is nothing other than the pure acceptance of the will of the Eternal.

Have we explained the mystery of the prayer of petition? No, we have only found in its mystery once more the mystery of everything Christian. That alone is our explanation. However, it suffices for faith. Just as there is truly heaven and truly earth, just as there is truly a living, free, almighty God and also a truly free, creaturely person, thus there is this duality even in the prayer of petition: the true cry of need that wants the earthly, and true, radical capitulation of man before the God of judgment and incomprehensibilities. And both in one? One without canceling the other? Yes. How is that possible? As possible as there is Christ. Realized, however, thousands of times in that true Christian life in which one becomes—Oh highest deed of man— like a child that is not afraid of being a child or even childish because it knows its Father is wiser and more farsighted and kind in his inexplicable harshness. And therefore the child doesn't make his childlike judgment and craving the final authority. To be a child before God in midst of the death, agony, and despair that is felt and suffered. To be a composed, modest, quiet, trusting child during the plunge into the extreme emptiness of the entire human being up to death, yes, death on the cross. To be both in one and thus to pray both into his prayer of petition: anxiety and trust, the will for life and the readiness for death, the certainty of being heard and the complete forswearing of being heard according to one's own plan. That is the mystery of Christian life and of the Christian prayer of petition. For Christ the God-man is the one and only law for both.

Who understands this apology for the prayer of petition? Only he who prays. If you want to understand it: pray, beg, weep. Beg for the necessities of the body so that your petition for the earthly gift transforms you more and more into a heavenly human being. Beg so that you make yourself into an offering to above during the petition for the gift from above. Beg so that your continuing prayer of petition appears to be a pledge of your faith in the light of God in the darkness of the world, for your hope for life in this constant dying, for your loyalty of love that loves without reward.

We are underway, wanderers between two worlds. Because we are still wandering on earth, let us ask for what we need on this earth. Since, however, we are pilgrims of eternity on this earth, let us not forget that we don't want to be heard as if we had a permanent abode, as if we didn't know that we have to enter the life that, through downfall and death, is the goal of life and prayer in all petitions.

As long as our hands remain folded, remain folded even in the most horrifying downfall, that is how long the benevolence and the life of God surrounds us—invisibly and mysteriously, but truly—and all the plunges into horror and into death are only a falling into the abysses of eternal love.

6

Prayers of Consecration

In the private and public prayer life of the Catholic Christian of today, there is a form of prayer which, as far as we know, is of fairly recent date in this contemporary form of expression. However, it has now become so frequent that it is probably worth the effort to reflect upon it. We mean "prayers of consecration." Everyone has at least heard in church of the consecration of the world to the heart of the Savior during the feast of the Most Sacred Heart of Jesus or of Christ the King. These and similar prayer formulas have become common. There is a similar consecration to the Immaculate Heart of the Blessed Virgin. A "consecration of the family" to the heart of the Savior is recommended. A bishop "consecrates" his diocese to a patron saint or to the Blessed Virgin and her heart. The members of the Congregation of Mary "consecrate" themselves to their heavenly patron, and so on. Naturally such prayers of consecration can have a very diverse sense and a varying significance depending on the context in which such a consecration occurs, on the person it is directed to, or on the people or the congregations which undertake them. We want—at least at first—to quite neglect these essential differences, similarly the official and liturgical functions in which some of these consecrations occur. We only want to consider very generally those "consecrations" that are composed in a prayer in which the one consecrating carries out the act of his own heart silently and simply as a personal responsibility, he "consecrates" himself.

But *what* actually *happens* during a consecration? We know from the start that a consecration is not a resolution and not a vow. In a resolution, "we intend to do something." What we intend to do may be something decreed or advised by God. But we improve *ourselves*, we are dealing with ourselves, while in a consecration we look away from ourselves to the person to whom we are consecrating ourselves, and the movement of our heart passes away from us over to another. In a vow, we promise God a certain achievement while assuming a new, strict obligation on ourselves. This achievement to which we obligate ourselves is certainly great and significant, and as a final result is supposed to transfer someone over to the holy love of God, and thus in vows a consecration of a human being to God may also be included as the ultimate end of vows. However, its immediate content is the acceptance of an obligation for a clearly defined, objective achievement. Consecration, however, goes directly from heart to heart. It is not the application of a mode of love, of a work in which, as in a resolution and a vow, love is supposed to grow and prove itself, rather it is the free streaming of love itself from person to person, from heart to heart.

However, if this is so, then the original question is raised once more: Does something happen during a consecration, something new? Doesn't the Christian already stand in this love and under its commandment which has always required not just an achievement, a work, but rather man himself, his innermost heart, totally for God? Without considering that consecration doesn't always aim directly at God himself and our Lord, can we do something more than just tell God again, and again and again, what we are already doing, what we have to do with or without consecration, namely that we love him? Is consecration more than an echo in words of that soundless movement of the Holy Spirit that bears us gently and inexorably and takes us into God? And if we say that a consecration doesn't mean a new obligation, don't we have to say this because every obligation, the old one and the new one, is always encompassed and surpassed by the duty which is more than a duty, through the love that demands everything from us and is only fulfilled when it does not set itself a duty-bound measure, but rather gives away our whole heart from our whole heart, the loving heart, not the heart fulfilling a duty?

Let's be careful and cautious at this point. We said that consecration only states what has always been our duty and the act of our heart: I love you, my God! Does nothing really happen through this word? Obviously this question must be correctly understood from the outset. We mean the word that the heart and not only the mouth speaks, the word that is spoken seriously and with concentration, maturely and upon reflection, that is not just a frivolous word of the everyday (there is also a religious everyday), but rather "ex-presses"[1] us ourselves, takes us completely along so that we ourselves become "stated" and "promised." Doesn't anything happen through this word? On the contrary, everything can happen through it although everything may seem to remain unchanged. In order to comprehend that, we shall have to expand the scope a bit further.

The spiritual life of man, through which he strives for his ultimate goal in the perfection of his free nature in the possession of God, is not just an exterior chain of acts lined up together in time in which the second must delete the first, must force it out of reality in order to be itself until it has to vacate the field of existence to the third act. Rather, in the moment of human presence, man's past is always mysteriously present. Man as spiritual person acts (or at least is able to act) in every moment from the total sum of his past. His past is "preserved," that is, sustained, as it were, in an extract, that is, in the spiritual physiognomy that came to be present in freedom in the experience of life, and so forth, of man. As in the case of a bullet in flight, its location at any moment can only be determined from the total sum of the path it has already traveled. As in the mysterious timbre of a priceless violin that has just been played, everything that has ever been played on it by the artist mysteriously resonates, as it were. That's how even more in every present action of man, his entire past, his knowledge that has been gained with great effort and pain, his depth of life's experience of the shocks of his existence, the pleasure and the pain of his entire past life (even if under quite different omens), are drawn in and impart to this momentary act its entire direction of movement, its draft and resonance. The past is really maintained and preserved in the present. Or let us say, it can be, should be. Man can and should go back and bring his past into the present moment during his free decision of the moment. Everything that he was, he *is*, and he can and

1. Translator's note: *aus-spricht.*

should fill the new moment with the entire weight of this I. He should not only grasp the possibilities of his existence, which are presented temporally one after another in freedom, correctly endure them, and make them into "the eternal in man." He should also endure every moment of the soundlessly present fullness of his spiritual history which remains for him as a spiritual person as the ever more enriched possibility of his respective present.

But more still. Man can anticipate his future during an act of spiritual decision occurring now in grace—that is even more mysterious but nonetheless true. Not only or exclusively in what we call resolution, pre-planning, decision making, preconsideration and their forms such as promises, vows, and the like. In this man can already foresee the future in his life. However, resolutions and similar spiritual occurrences are things of the present that, no matter how important they may be for the future of man, actually are only important for the future of man if they are accomplished not now but later, and this accomplishment doesn't depend on a present but a future decision. When we say that we can mysteriously anticipate the future in an act occurring now, then we don't just mean the development of facts that we can't change once they have occurred and which therefore are of unavoidable significance for our future decisions regardless of how they fall. Such facts exist and are of greater or lesser importance. If someone has married another human being, if someone is ordained a priest, if someone has lived and thus used up for good a segment of his life which was granted to him only once and can't be repeated, then he has created facts in his life which are significant for every future act and decision. Every future action will have to come to terms with these facts. Man can no longer act as if these facts had not occurred. However—and that is just as important—man can come to terms with these facts in the future in entirely *different* ways, assign entirely different characteristics to them later. For example, he can later stand by his earlier decision to love *or* betray it. He can always invest his whole life in his vocation as a priest *or* live out his life apart from it, indeed even be unfaithful to it on the exterior. Therefore, as much as both opposite decisions are not able to get around the fact created earlier, then two (or many) opposite possibilities are still given even after the free arrangement of such facts, and then the future is still open and undetermined. Therefore, this spiritual phenomenon is not yet what we mean when we say the present moment, under certain circumstances, can include the future.

In order to explain that and how such a thing is possible, we want to consider an objection that seems to demonstrate that such a thought is impossible. The fact of freedom seems to demonstrate that such an idea cannot be carried out. Man is always free. Therefore in the future moments of his life also. As a result, it seems to be incompatible with this fact that man could bring his future into the present moment in anticipation so that he could make a decision about it, fill the current moment with the weight of his future, as it were, anticipating the possibilities of what is still in the future in order to let them become reality in this moment. It seems that one could also apply the biblical word here: "Each day has enough trouble of its own."[2] One thing results from this objection as an important insight which must not be forgotten in the following considerations. If we disregard marginal cases for now, which must be briefly touched upon later, then it follows from the fact of freedom that stretches through all of man's life that the free decision of a moment cannot control the future, so that man *knows* for certain and concretely by this one act that he has stamped his entire future and has control over it. For otherwise the future would only be the almost mechanical unfolding of what had already occurred in such a moment. Future life would no longer stand in the dark of the incalculable future and under the law of responsible risk. There may be cases, as the history of the saints and theology teach, in which a person knows (theology speaks of the known "confirmed in grace")[3] that his life has actually progressed so far before God as free and total decision that it will no longer fail to succeed. However, as mentioned, those are marginal cases that won't concern us further here because they are infrequent, and we won't have to reckon with them in our own lives. In those, man already knows that he, as a spiritual person, has, so to speak, already died the blessed death of the just.

---

2. Translator's note: Matt 6:34.
3. Translator's note: *Befestigung der Gnade,* cf. *confirmatio in gratia.*

In general, this knowing of how one actually stands before God will not converge with the freedom and the dark of the earthly pilgrimage—which is decided in the dark—the unknowing. However, if in general a *known* state-of-having-made-a-decision about the future doesn't exist, then the question hasn't been answered yet of whether there could be an attempted and successful, although in its success not certainly known, decisive anticipation of the future or not. But such a phenomenon seems to be quite possible. For first, freedom in its actual sense is not, as the everyday impression might imply, the capability of being able to do every single thing in every moment (at least in the inner yes and no of the spiritual core of the person). On the contrary, freedom is the capability to be able to express oneself freely once and entirely, the capability to be able to create freely *final* facts, so that freedom doesn't deny the possibility of creating *inner* (not only outer as those we had observed above) facts forever but has its final sense therein. For the non-free creates conditions which are always variable, reversible, and revisable. Freedom, on the other hand, equals the ultimate, unrepeatable, and eternal. For just this reason, the ultimate, eternal, lasting destiny of the spiritual person is not a condition that befalls the free person unexpectedly and against the tendency of freedom, cutting the latter off from the outside and rendering it impossible, but rather is the maturity and result of freedom itself. And, therefore, the free decision in every moment of its own accord anticipates the entirety of life. Therefore one can decide his entire eternity in one moment. Therefore freedom seeks in every moment, in which it is really at work, the total stamping of the person, its pure and full self-expression in which the act of freedom becomes the ultimate condition of the person, the enduring act of the person. This tendency of freedom in the moment to become not just a single moment of self-preserving temporality but rather the moment of eternity, wherein one's whole life is composed and decided, may not succeed for a thousand times in the individual case. The success of this tendency for man (as is actually the case) may depend on exterior conditions that simply don't come under the control of this freedom. The person may not succeed in a thousand cases in trying to include the entire possibility of its spiritual life in the moment in order to make out of a thousand connected acts of temporality the one and total actuality of one life. However, this tendency exists because it belongs to the essence of freedom. The freedom of the moment always grasps at the totality of life, is always responsible for the totality of life, for its time and eternity. Factually it usually won't grasp the entirety, in a thousand cases it will slip away, whether because the act of freedom itself isn't radical, that is, rooted enough, to reach into the depth of human existence, or whether because the exterior preconditions, which are independent of the freedom of man, are not given in the full extent. Freedom will never (or almost never) know with that knowledge, which we normally call it and which we only can grasp reflexively, whether it has really succeeded with the act of total decision. However, there can be one such moment when freedom really effects what it actually always wants: to decide about everything at once and for ever. There is *one* such moment for certain: death. There at least not just the thread of life will be cut off by the Fates, a thread which the person would have continued to spin (as if it wanted to spin it endlessly!). At least there man has (although we never know how this happens, we even have necessarily and unavoidably the opposite impression) by himself completed the melody of his life, there he dies his "own" death, that is, at least in the moment of death he is what he has made himself freely and finally, so that the factual result of his life and that which he himself freely and finally wants to be are the same. *When*, however, does this moment of dying exactly occur insofar as it is an act of freedom itself, that is, of completing oneself from inside, *when* has man done himself? What we just said about death is only correct in the sense that (according to the testimony of faith), at least during death as the biological cessation of life, this moment of dying that completes itself in freedom has occurred. However, we don't know whether this moment coincides temporally with death as a biological cessation of life. We can only say that we don't know as long as we live (leaving aside the marginal cases mentioned above) whether this moment has already occurred, that we therefore always have to reckon with the moment of complete control over ourselves being ahead of us. However, we can sense also that it doesn't coincide always or perhaps not even frequently with death in the usual sense. The observation of the average death, from the state of insensibility to unconsciousness, doesn't seem to speak for such a coincidence. We said, however, that every free act always wants to be the act of such self-fulfilling self-expression of the total kind. However, then we can sense that this act falls perhaps in quite another exterior point in time than just in the moment of the biological cessation of life, and if it is actually the goal of every act of freedom, we must want to do it always.

Aren't there also experiences of man that point in this direction, that up to now have been determined a priori from the essence of freedom? Haven't we experienced moments in the history of our soul during which we had the impression that we could never forget them, that the attitude, the experience, the state of mind which existed then, could never disappear from our being because it was so deeply engraved in the countenance of our spirit that we could never go back from what happened in us in freedom, not although it was free but precisely because it was free? If we are already older, hasn't it appeared to us quietly and shyly but in unspeakable rapture, so that one doesn't even dare to admit it to oneself, as if we had the impression that we could no longer elude the love of God, that the divine Hunter had already surrounded his game that always wants to escape from him, so that it can only wait in blissful trembling for the moment when it finally becomes his catch? (We must not forget that such experiences of grace in one are also acts of our freedom that happened in the yes of our inner being.) And even when such experiences turn out to be illusions in individual cases (as the hiker has during a mountain hike when he thinks he's close to his destination because a segment of his path is removed from his view of the rest of the way). Aren't such illusions in individual cases a proof that what is intended exists, that the spirit (how could it otherwise fall for such an illusion in individual cases?) presses toward such moments when everything is totally completed and thus that really—suddenly and unexpectedly and without causing a commotion—happens which it craves: to have the fullness of one's entire life until the end in one moment and in freedom to form it into ultimate perfection? That's how it is: In freedom we always grasp for the whole of our life. Innumerable times our grasp will only catch a part of the whole; but we will try again and again to gather together the past and the future in the one act of freedom in order to form out of everything the ultimate truth and reality of our life. And at some time our life's hour of destiny occurs (only God clearly hears its tolling): Unexpectedly and hidden from ourselves, we suddenly shall have the fruit of the whole of life entirely in our hand. Whatever still happens temporally in our life is only the blissful finale of a symphony that delights because it can't be any different. It's like the final count of an election, the result of which is pretty much known, like the final ripening of a fruit which has already fallen from the tree.

In order to inform ourselves briefly, let's call this momentous hour of our freedom, the unique and disguised, the moment of eternity in time, the moment of temporal eternity. We now can sense what this moment is. We know that this moment as such remains hidden to us (although done in freedom), but also that freedom is always pressing toward it and only will be fulfilled in it, that we, whether we know it or not, always live in the attempt to attain this moment, to fulfill it and us in it.

We have only sought to determine this moment of eternity in time according to its abstract, formal character and describe it as the act of freedom's total self-control over man and the possibilities of his entire life. With that, however, not much has been said. For this total self-control as an act of freedom can be this way *or* that way, it can be yes *or* no, rise or fall, salvation or perdition, the eternity of the saved or the eternity of the lost in time. Therefore we have to ask further: What must this moment of eternity in time be filled with so that it can be the eternity of salvation, the pure and ultimate yes? What is the act by which alone the whole man can soar *properly* into true eternity? The answer is obvious: the act of the love of God. But don't let us hold this simple answer for too self-evident! Because it is not, in two respects.

If we have understood what we considered up to now, then one thing is apparent: Not every act of the love of God is a moment of eternity in time. Each one may be an attempt at it. But not only shall we never (or only in the most infrequent cases) know whether this attempt to accomplish this moment as an act of love has succeeded, rather, these attempts will fail in all but one case. (That naturally does not at all mean that these "failed" attempts would be meaningless before God and for us. They are extremely important, unavoidably necessary exercises for the one and successful attempt.) For such a moment has only transpired (that was the reason for all this talking) in the act of love when the act in it happened with *all* our heart, with all our soul, with all our mind, and with all our strength. Therefore only when man has totally (and then and therefore ultimately and irrevocably) consumed himself in the act of loving freedom. However, in this way the act of our love will only be infrequent (indeed only once, but then for ever). For when have we ever loved God with all our heart, with all our soul, with all our mind, and with all our strength (Mark 12:30)? If we were to take these frightening words "whole" and "all" quite seriously, we could even say: The commandment to love God with the totality of man (therefore of his nature and of his time) is the commandment to love for this moment of eternity in time, to always attempt it anew until it is granted to us in grace and succeeds. It is the commandment of love in the moment of temporal eternity. Every moment of love tends toward this moment, becomes fulfilled in it; however, it is not always this moment already.

In a second respect, it is not so self-evident that this love and it alone (if ever an act of man) is the content of the proper moment of eternity in time. This moment is supposed to be the moment of integration of our entire life. However, is it so self-evident that love, and it alone, is capable of achieving this integration, or does the not at all so self-evident and familiar nature of love become thereby clear to us?

When we ask what is the basic act of man in which he can totally gather his whole nature and life, that can encompass everything, that can comprehend everything in itself, everything that means man and human life, laughing and crying, bliss and despair, spirit and heart, the everyday and the hours of destiny, heaven and earth, compulsion and freedom, sin and redemption, past and future, then the answer is not so self-evident.

But nonetheless it is really so: The love of God is able to encompass everything and only this love alone. It alone places man before him without whom man would only be the dreadful consciousness of radical emptiness and nothingness. It alone is capable of uniting all the powers of man, the manifold and chaotic and self-contradicting, because it directs all of them to God whose

unity and infinity can create in man that unity that unites the
multiplicity of the finite without destroying it. Love alone lets
man forget himself (what a hell if we couldn't succeed in that).
It alone can redeem the darkest hours of the past, for it alone
finds the courage to believe in the mercy of our holy God. It
alone doesn't keep everything for itself and thus can control the
future (which otherwise man is always tempted to save up for
himself in his anxiety about his finitude which he has to handle
sparingly). Together with God it can also love this earth (and
thus in it also integrate all earthly love into the moment of eternity), and only it will never lose courage because it loves him
who never regretted the risk of such an earth of guilt, of the
curse, of death and futility. The love for God is really the single,
total integration of human existence, and we have only comprehended it in its majesty and dignity and all-encompassing mag-
nitude if we have understood it as that, if we realize that it must
be the content of the moment of temporal eternity, because
without it this moment would be nothing other than the judgment already carried out in secret (John 3:18), and because con-
versely only it can be in this moment what it wants to be and
must be: everything.

There is still a great deal that could be said about this act of
love in the moment of temporal eternity. Above all that such an
act is grace in spite of how much it must be called the most sublime act of freedom. Precisely because we can only love God in
his power, precisely because our love is always just an answer to
him who loved us first, because he must pour out his love into
our hearts through the Holy Spirit who is given to us, therefore
this moment is grace. This moment, however, is grace beyond
the universal grace-ness of our love of God because the moment
of temporal eternity as such is grace. For to be able to control
oneself entirely, to receive control over the extreme depths of
one's possibilities, to be able to totally liquefy the "ore" of life so
that it can be used totally and slag-free in the casting of the one
image of God, this possibility as one given immediately and always belongs to the nature of an angel. It is, however, not given
to man permanently and always at his disposal but rather is only
the supreme moment of his life, which is granted to him from
grace if it is given to him just *so* that he *properly* fulfills it and en-

dures it. Therefore it is grace that he receives it and again grace that he can fulfill it with love for God. The supreme moment of freedom, in which it creates its finality in the eternal integration of one's entire life, is grace and freedom according to its nature and existence.

We seem to have strayed far from our question of what actually happens in a consecration. However, we are quite close to our goal. For we can now simply say: Consecration (as we described it at the beginning) is the serious, collected attempt of the moment of eternity in time as the act of love. If we recall what we wanted to understand by the moment of temporal eternity, the act of total and ultimate integration of our entire life, and when we quite simply and without bias look at what man undertakes to do in a consecration, then we shall probably recognize the given definition of consecration as correct, and it needs only a few words of explanation.

That the basic act of consecration is the act of love should not need further proof. That such an act of love in a consecration is attempted as pure and full of clarity, full of earnestness and with the entire strength of the heart in all "sincerity" (that is, in the unity of all powers of the spirit and the mind), that is probably just as directly readable from what happens in the exterior process of consecration. Otherwise what are the preparation, the consideration, the expressiveness, and solemnity of a consecration supposed to mean? It has already been said in enough detail that an act of love of this kind by its nature strives to bring about the moment of temporal eternity, because it is only in this moment that love with the whole heart, with the entirety of man (what it wants to be when it takes place so solemnly), and this attempt at it can possibly succeed. *If* the attempt of consecration succeeds, then that moment of eternity in time occurs that is the decisive event of our life before the eyes of God, that act to which our past life strived toward a goal in a mysterious teleology as its preparation and of which everything following is only as the accomplishment of an ultimate and irrevocable theme.

Certainly the attempt will frequently not succeed or not quite succeed, certainly we shall never know whether it succeeded, and thus even after the consecration we shall still have to try further to effect our salvation in fear and trembling in the awareness that we are not yet what we are supposed to be and are able to be and that the pilgrimage of our life will still be distant and full of un-expected surprises. But isn't consecration already holy and great as an *attempt* of this kind at an hour of destiny? And who knows, perhaps the attempt has been successful; perhaps the one great word of our life has been said in it, really has been said by *us*, the word in which we have totally and ultimately expressed our-selves? We don't know. But God knows. Isn't that enough? Isn't it odd about love that it says new words again and again, more concentrated, more sincere words, until it has found the one word that really says everything and is worthy to become eternal?

From this point of our consideration, perhaps a few things could be clarified concerning the *manner* in which a consecra-tion should be undertaken: how it cannot be an everyday event of our religious life; how it has to be prepared; how its concrete type must correspond to the spiritual and mental characteristics of the one being consecrated so that it can be possible for the heart to go along with the words of the consecration; how it is absurd to multiply the number of consecrations into the unfore-seeable; how man should attempt it with a genuine, serious, re-alistic visualization of his entire life; how it must be prayed for as grace; and so on. However, we can't go any further into these questions here.

We began our considerations with the question whether some-thing really happens in a consecration. We can now answer this question emphatically: Consecration is the attempt to do *every-thing*, the attempt to accomplish the total act of life. If this attempt succeeds, then not just "something" but everything has happened. If the attempt doesn't entirely succeed, still, an inexpressibly great deal has happened: A human being has realized at least a part of love which in any case is the task of his life and content of his eter-nity. Isn't that a great deal? And even if one can say that this also happens in the everyday of Christian life, there above all because the drabness and bitterness of the everyday is the genuine situation of true love. Then the reply to that is once more: Yes, certainly, when the everyday is really love. And if this is not easy and self-ev-ident, then isn't it good and salutary to do it, *whatever* should hap-pen, more decisively and with more reflection? This happens during consecration even when it doesn't succeed in being the perfect love of the moment of eternity in time. Therefore everything, or a great deal, happens during consecration.

If, up to now, we have considered consecration from the vantage point of man, then one naturally could ask the question whether "something happens" in it also from God's perspective; how he replies to the word of love during a consecration and whether the actual thing that occurs in a consecration is therein. Certainly there would be something to say about that. For the Bible says (Jas 4:8) that whoever draws near to God, God draws near to him. And so a great deal would have to be said about the splendor of God's drawing near in a consecration. However, the decisive part for our context has already been said. For he draws near to us by giving us the grace-filled possibility to draw near to him. However, what that means was always the point of our discussion.

A final question must be touched upon briefly. Up to now in our considerations, we have simply presupposed that consecration is directed to *God*, to the Father, the triune God, to the God-man love of the Lord and his heart. For we have spoken of the love of God in its supreme moment. This, however, by its very nature addresses itself to God. However, there are also consecrations which, at least in their immediate content of meaning, are not addressed to God but to a saint in heaven and above all to the Blessed Virgin and Mother of God. Does what we have said up to now apply to this type of consecration also? To this we can reply that it does, at least when its sense is correctly understood. A consecration, and the love for a human being in the blessed community of the saints in heaven which is activated in it, are in their deepest content of being an act of the love of God. For love of neighbor (and thus of those who are really closest to us because they are eternally connected with God) is "for the sake of God," is born by the theological virtue of the love of God. Why and how that is cannot and does not have to be explained here. We may presuppose this principle as a universal doctrine of theology. If we consecrate ourselves to a heavenly human being, the movement of our heart doesn't go to him in order to end with him, but rather it goes to him, as it were, right through him in order to soar further into God with the movement of his heart which has become eternity (indeed, we love him precisely because he has it). That applies above all to the consecration to the Blessed Virgin and her "heart" (that is, the quintessence of her love of God which has become eternity, the symbol of the sincere wholeness of her pure nature which belongs totally to God). Whoever consecrates himself to this love and really knows what he is doing and what the act of his heart is moving toward in such a consecration, he must be drawn into the eternal movement of love of the heart of the Virgin. He must love God and finally consecrate himself to him.

There are many prayers of consecration. Many have already been prayed for and over us. And perhaps they seemed a little too frequent, were said a little too quickly, and perhaps were a little embarrassing because they seemed to grasp too courageously for the highest words when our heart was able to follow with difficulty or not at all. Indeed, it may appear as if even the one who truly loves God is still silent before God about his love and lets the bitter desire for a love that one doesn't find in oneself talk mutely before him rather than to declare impudently to the inexorable Searcher of hearts that one loves him (oh, if one only knew that for sure?). However, our loving God indeed knows about the need of our poor heart, and he still loves (that is the divine thing of *his* love) the love in us which is not worthy of him, he still loves the mute pain of the powerless heart that believes it is not able to love, not truly to love. If God is so, then isn't a piece of unredeemed pride in this mute modesty and in the anxiety of speaking to God unself-consciously as a child about one's love for him as if our love actually would have to be worthy of him, as if he only would love us if our love is as it is supposed to be? However, if we give up this hidden pride, can't we then say to him—shyly and seriously as a child—Dear Father, I—yes, I'll risk it—I love you? All prayers of consecration are only variations of this one and inexhaustible theme.

7

The Prayer of Guilt

"This, then, is how you should pray: 'Our Father . . ., forgive us our guilt' . . . !" When the Christian has learned from the Lord how to pray he prays the prayer for forgiveness of his guilt[1] before God; he always prays this way. Daily and every day anew. He doesn't just pray *pro forma* the plea for forgiveness of a debt from *earlier*—when he was not yet converted, had not yet done penance, perhaps had not yet been hallowed by the forgiveness of all sins in the rebirth of the new man in baptism with water and the Spirit. He pleads for the forgiveness of his guilt, which weighs heavily upon him *now*, always and anew.

Can we really do that? Aren't we the redeemed who are supposed to appear redeemed: the cheerful heirs of the holy ones in light, reborn children of the Father shining like stars in a dark world, children of mercy, the new people, the heirs of the promise? And still simpler, more concrete, and more everyday: Do we feel so guilty that we can beat our breast every day "in the spirit of repentance and with contrite heart:"[2] Lord, have mercy on me a poor sinner?

Certainly the Christian of today generally experiences his personally becoming a Christian *after* his baptism. Baptism marks the beginning of his life, the evidence of the Lord's mercy marks

1. Translator's note: The German word used in the title and throughout this chapter is *Schuld*, which means both debt and guilt in English. Rahner uses *Schuld* in both senses as well as its root in various verbal and adjectival forms throughout the chapter.

2. Translator's note: Cf. Ps 51:7.

the beginning of the paths of his life before it has even begun. And whoever knows what is God's and what is man's will find that justified. But with that the course, the struggle, and the challenge by the powers of darkness are not taken away from man. It is not spared him, rather it is the lofty and decisive task of his life to become what he has been since baptism, a Christian. However, that means encountering God with spirit and heart in the decision of his inmost being, the God of annihilating majesty, the God of judging justice, the God of incomprehensible mercy and grace, the God who shone in the countenance of Jesus, who made himself known on the cross and in that human being who sits at the right hand of the Father and pours out his Holy Spirit over all flesh. And in this drama of the encounter between God and man—that doesn't begin until after the child's baptism and is decided over an eternity—there can be an act, even for baptized Christians, in which he wanders far from God in the vanity of his heart, is a man of the earth, flesh, a "decent" man perhaps, very proper (who never comes in conflict with the police or cheap, everyday morality which is, oh, so tolerant), who, however, doesn't sense anything of the consuming holiness of God, who guiltily-innocently transgresses God's commandment from which life and death depend, prescribes to God how seriously, that is, unseriously, he has to take what makes up the life of man: the storm and stress of youth, and in mature age the compromises between what one is supposed to be and what one thinks one unavoidably "must" be are compelled by the reality of life. The years when one suddenly notices ("I don't know myself how it happened") that one had "grown away" from the Church's Christianity, when faith, etc., simply "weren't there" anymore. One thinks, with a shrug of the shoulders, of being able to determine it as a fact that took place but wasn't the result of a decision. However, then the next act in this drama may have taken place (the one that occurred in old times *before* baptism): the grace of God, which is judgment, befalls man, exposes him, shows him who he is (he had known it "basically"—namely in the bottom of his denied heart—all along), a sinner who, in his earlier life, loved the darkness more than the light, who gently and without ado, quietly, quietly (one mustn't notice anything), quite incidentally bent the norms of his conscience so that they no longer provided any direction, for whom it was basically all right no matter what he became (without his doing it of course), who (as one in a "dream"—what can I do about it?—turns off the alarm clock to oversleep innocently) noiselessly was fleeing from God (oh, one can't stand being with him; that is the manifest proof that he doesn't exist or is to be imagined quite differently from that one from whom one is fleeing). The more man seemed to be at one with himself before, the more this seems no longer to be a proof of his prior good conscience (although it may have been "objectively" in error, even the impenitent admits this as a possible possibility) now under the judging light of God, but rather as proof of how deeply his free, truly culpable sin started at the core of his being; indeed, so deeply that nothing more in his interior raised an audible objection; that he doesn't acknowledge as an exoneration for his earlier life the fact that he didn't always have this "light" but rather as evidence against himself *how* much he loved the darkness—so that he no longer saw this light that shines on every man—and as evidence of the incomprehensible grace of God. Perhaps such a one protested for a while; perhaps he "defended" his "good conscience" for a time; perhaps he even turned this new light into a complaint against God: "Why didn't you show me that earlier?" instead of confessing that *he* didn't want to see it. Perhaps he still tried to save a "uniformly" common thread throughout his life without having to reject it in condemnation (even if he now "had come to other, better, new insights") by attempting excuses: he meant well although it didn't always turn out that way; indeed he had changed but always acted in accordance with the new law to which he "actually" had never been unfaithful. But when the sweet and burning light of God which is the truth of God (not of man) and love inexorably (Oh grace of God, incalculable!) and judgingly shines further, then man gives way. No, then man becomes strong. He finds (how should he be able to do it on his own?) the courage to let go of himself, the innermost center of his falsely determined freedom, to reject it, to agree with the judge who condemns him (he knows that this court is the mercy of God), to admit that he is a sinner: a sinner, a debtor, not one who didn't know better up to now, not one who finally came to a better insight in the course of his development, not one who always meant well in his deepest heart. Rather, a sinner: one who meant evil in his deepest heart. One who kept the official books of his so-called good conscience, which only he himself read by day so that nothing incriminating was evident (however, they had been falsified, falsified by him, he admits that now). A sinner who forgot (oh yes, naturally "accidentally forgot") because he did not want to know that his evil heart betrayed the good grounds of reason ("the intellectual difficulties"), which could not deal with its assessment because it had basically allied itself with the bookkeeping for a long time before the individual charges came in and payment was demanded. A sinner who carried out moral rearguard actions so that his capitulation didn't need to be admitted as a clear case of cowardice. A sinner who gladly let the birds of these times steal God's seed out of the soil of his heart because basically he readily wanted to be dispensed from bearing fruit. A sinner who was so smart that the principles of his morality (even if they had to be supplied through "divine illumination") always harmonized famously with what one wanted to do at that moment. Someone who could even say to God: Guide me, but not away from doing this; who acted like the "respectable" girl: "I'll do it—as long as you keep my conscience clear by forcing me." My God, if someone under your light admits that this mystery of evil has taken place in his heart, if he admits it without asking how it is possible but rather confessing that he himself did it, if, while talking to you, he doesn't "change the subject" like the woman at Jacob's well away from his *own* guilt to universal guiltiness. If your grace makes it possible that the sinner breaks away from himself (what still remains "he" if he separates himself from himself when "he" is so guilty that he—the whole man—deserves to be thrown into hell with body and soul, and you wouldn't do this if a good spark didn't remain in him?). What a miracle of your grace that doesn't declare an "upheaval" in a person's structure. Then he truly flees from himself to you. Then he takes your side against himself, then he no longer asserts himself but rather your holy splendor, then he is with you (borne over the abyss by your grace), and his judgment of himself is your mercy for him, then he loves you (how could he be able to hate himself if he didn't love you?). Then the simple miracle of all miracles takes place that man loves your holy love more, although, no, because it is yours, than his own closed I in which he sat imprisoned in the dark. Then he really prays: Father, before you and against you have I sinned, forgive me my guilt!

Such prayer exists. However, is the question which we were dealing with resolved? The question whether the honest and the redeemed can daily say the prayer of guilt? Is the issue resolved for *all* of us and for each one everyday? Well, one could say that whoever was redeemed out of the darkness, for which he himself was guilty, into the light which is God's, will say his *mea culpa* again and again, which is the form in which the redeemed, the unfettered and happy sinner, confesses his love to God. For when God gives his grace, it remains his, and the truly graced one, the pure one, the loving redeemed one never claims it—that was given as a gift and is the godly splendor of his new life—as his own as if it were his by right and self-evidence. Grace remains grace which always depends on the eternally new miracle from God's love which can never be separated as a thing from this free inclination of God's heart. And only as grace is it the new life of man. Grace only as long as it is received as the pardoning kiss of God's forgiveness, grace only as long as man seemingly were lifted up by God anew (anew? in the old way? always? what does the consequence of time have to do in this act that controls an *entire* life?) out of the dark depths of his guilt as if in a continuous, floating transferral. I always call myself a sinner (one could say, as a variation on Augustine), man always says, because you always say to me: Child of my love. And as your *creative* word punishes my lying (your child, Oh God, is no sinner), but it is your truth, not my truth, then it is true only as long as I confess *my* truth to you constantly: Lord, have mercy on me! Perhaps the question is actually answered this way. But in order that we comprehend it, first several things have to be said and then expanded upon.

When one asks tradition (or at least superficially interrogates it), one could reply to our question: The good Christian prays daily for the forgiveness of his daily mistakes and weaknesses. But these have not separated him from God, he lives even with these sins as God's child and housemate. But nevertheless even these "venial" sins are sins. If a miracle of grace doesn't happen, then he falls into them seven times a day and therefore even the "holy ones" can say, not only humbly but in truth—*veraciter et humiliter*:[3] Forgive us our guilt, as an ancient council already stated. That is all true, but is this truth everything? Not as if one would take the "light," the "venial" sins lightly, as if the matter were not weighty enough to ask for their forgiveness because they are "light." We shall soon have to say why and how gravely the Christian has to take light sins (the moralists say *leve*[4] correctly, but that is frighteningly curious). But is the daily prayer of the Christian, the good Christian in the state of grace, sufficiently explained this way? Can he really speak *as such* from the *bottom* of his heart: Forgive me my guilt (He even says, my greatest guilt!), can he honestly say that (oh, one can even be dishonest in this direction and say many and great words in prayer that the Lord loathes)? For let us presuppose it has to do with really venial sins (and let us presuppose, as the Church always teaches, that such exist), then it is simply true that such don't arise from the innermost core of man where he is completely at one, completely he himself, and where he therefore decides about himself and his eternal destiny; that they, on the other hand, are somehow more external (as "traitorous" as they may be for the interior and thus they may have been "entirely voluntary" in the sense of a formal freedom). But then one cannot repent them "more innerly" as such in truth, one cannot take them to heart more deeply than they themselves were. Repentance as countermovement of the heart against venial sins strictly as such cannot arise more centrally in the core of the person, cannot be existentially more radical than the venial sins were and "deserve" it. The attempt to take them more seriously leads to dishonesty or a harmful overloading of the soul's possibilities or to an underestimation of the gap between mortal and venial sin which is dangerous because it can lead man (who can never completely avoid venial sins and so somehow factually is "accustomed" to them) to not taking mortal sin, which he sees in a perspective with venial sin, more seriously than venial sin. (Whoever is familiar with the practice of some Christians during confession, with their

3. Translator's note: Latin, "truly and humbly."
4. Translator's note: Latin, "lightly."

constant, indiscriminate confession of mortal and venial sins, knows that this danger is not just the theoretical construction of self-righteous casuistic theology.) One can feel sorry for them (note that we are still only speaking provisionally about them as *such!*), one can improve them, one can see in them how little the (hopefully) final attitude toward God has grasped all of man and integrated all his instincts and chaotic drives into the one image of the new man. One can see in them the beginnings of a character development that give one cause to fear (also for salvation). One can measure with them the distance that still separates us from that goal where spirit and *flesh* rejoice in the blessed harmony of all-encompassing and all-melting love for God their healer.[5] One can reject them because they—as not positively integrable in the direction of the imperious call of God to him, the eternal and sole goal—are "against" the will of God, or as Thomas likes to say, they are "apart" from the will of God. One should seek to conquer the lack of zealous love of God which is expressed in them into a new elevation of the heart. But if we were to let the living word of God, "You are a sinner," penetrate for *their* sake like a double-edged sword even to the separation of spirit and soul, of marrow and bone, into the innermost heart, then this sharp word, which condemns our deepest sentiments, in this case would strike a place where *these* sins do not exist. No, the earnestness of the phrase "Forgive us our guilt," even when it's prayed by the reborn in spirit and in the tone in which the saints speak (with tears and in fear and trembling), is different from meaning just the "light" sins purely as such, just as moral theology understands them soberly and correctly and unavoidably but dangerously isolates them "abstractly" from the psychic-personal total phenomenon.

But what does the phrase mean if it can be spoken by the saints seriously but doesn't just mean the daily mistakes and

---

5. Translator's note: The word used here for this single occurrence in the text is *Heiland* (rather than *Erlöser,* "savior"). Until the advent of Norman French in England, the (Old) English cognate and equivalent was *Hælend,* "the healing one," "the one who heals," present active participle of the verb *halen,* "to heal," whence the modern English derivatives "hallow," "hail," "hale," "holy," "whole."

weaknesses, the tribute to the narrowness and limitation, to the lower instincts of man that are never quite integrated into man's final attitude?

Before we attempt to go beyond what has already been said to a more exact answer to this question, it has to be stated what kind of a Catholic doctrine on sin and justification *cannot* be meant when man always confesses being a sinner. Man can (as we have attempted to describe it) be found guilty by God of being a sinner, that he himself (this one here, just he, not man in general and everywhere) has sinned, has himself decided against God (naturally all the while not wanting to believe it by deceiving himself), that he himself, that singular I that is not able to hide itself behind anything, is not able to push the responsibility off to anything else, is not able to flee to a generality, he has done it, and no one else. That is the most horrible thing that can exist for this I because it itself, it wholly alone, inevitably has been found guilty, it cannot distance itself from this guilty one (unless it flees away from itself to God) and indeed is supposed to condemn itself. And therefore it attempts the most sublime cunning in order to save itself. In order to make the sin smaller, it makes it larger, so large that it becomes harmless again.

It doesn't say: *"I"* (without looking at each and everyone else) have sinned before you, I have *done* it. Rather it says: Yes, man (always and everywhere) is sinful, is sinful always and in everything, *is* radically evil, is this always and everywhere where he encounters you, Oh God, because he is man. He is different from you, evil, sinful, separated from you. Each and every one of us— and therefore I too—have always and everywhere—before we knew how we had begun—have always found ourselves to have decided against you. One is not able to escape this guilt (although it naturally would remain guilt), indeed its attempt would be the final hubris of man, who wants to justify himself before God by his own power, who does not want to confess that he is inevitably a sinner.

He makes the sin that he has committed in his own uniquely singular history—at one specific point, as his own decision, as his own responsibility—into a universal *constitutivum*[6] of his factual

6. Translator's note: Latin "construct."

being, into "original sin" (which in fact also exists, behind which, however, he may not hide his own sin), or into a type of a no longer astonishing manifestation of sinliness in general. He seemingly radicalizes sin, he makes it so general, he sets it so early on, so far back before the indissoluble *act* in reality of the unique I, so that he can very easily command everyone: Confess yourselves as sinners! But the individual is hiding in the choir of everyman, and whether one wants it or not, the confession of my own unique guilt is transformed into a lyrical, universal, minor-key lamentation on the *misère* of man.

But it is not so in truth. "My own" guilt exists so very much as the *act* of a unique individual, so very much the possibility of an Adamitic new guilt of the individual (as much as the son of Adam may share the burden of his father), that according to Catholic doctrine one may not only reckon with the possibility, but *must*, that this or that individual did *not* commit it, that everyone who has ever been justified must confess that he does not have to commit it, that he can avoid it, that when he nevertheless has committed it, *he* has *done* it, so much so that every "deeper" explanation of this "I have sinned" (not only "I am a sinner") is the beginning of a flight from the mystery of evil of one's own heart. What radical humiliation is here for the sin of man: *I* have committed it; not everyone is "basically like this" (not before God either); *not* just others have sinned, but rather *I*, I actually, always alone, and by myself. The only thing that man may lay claim to for "himself" is sin, his sin. And he must reject this one thing. Only then is he in the truth. Not until we have grasped this, accepted it, do we know what the creature is. One can only be like this when this "self-lessness" becomes possible by being devoured by the love for God.

Whenever this personal, unique guilt was not committed, whenever someone factually brings "the wedding garment of baptismal grace"[7] before the judgment seat of Christ, then this is all grace, pure, even greater grace. Not only because the grace of *divine* life, which is gifted to the creature, is always radically un-indebted,[8] not only because it is gifted to man who, as son of the

---

7. Translator's note: Cf. Gal 3:27; 2 Cor 5:3.
8. Translator's note: *ungeschuldet*.

sinful progenitor, certainly no longer had a claim to it, but the creature must thank the saving act of Christ alone; but also and above all because every decision in which the grace of God *could* be lost, in which man *could* act so that he would not inherit the kingdom of God, in which, however, he factually did not fall from the grace of his God, itself is the *grace* of God inasmuch as it is a right act of freedom effected by God. In this respect the not-having-sinned one is also one who has been saved by grace, one who is hovering over the abyss of his possible guilt over which he isn't holding himself but God is holding him (even if *his* holding is manifested in our freedom; why not? Or is our freedom ever so divine that God as the All-Efficient could only act when it disappears?). Inasmuch as the "one remaining in love from the beginning" (as Irenaeus said) is a pure hymn of praise to the glory of divine, incalculable grace, thus he is one who, like the most corrupt sinner, is always only with God by constantly fleeing to God and away from himself and the possibilities of a debt. "What do you have that you did not receive?"[9] The more he has, the more he is indebted to God for everything. And the purest innocence is the greatest debt to God. And this debt can only be paid with the praise of ineffably pure grace in which man confesses that everything is totally *his* work and nothing else: *sola gratia*.[10]

But if such human beings can exist (at least *can*)—no one knows (except for the case of the most humble handmaid and mother of the Savior) for certain whether and how many there really are, only God knows *how* he saves, if the salvation of each one is his and the mystery of his God—then how *can* everyone say, "I am a sinner," since no one is *allowed* to say that he has no sin?

If no one is allowed to say that he has no sin (no matter how 1 John 1:10 may be interpreted), must he then say, he has sin, he has *done* it? And if he doesn't find it? Is he then necessarily and always dishonest, an impenitent liar before God who doesn't want to confess and give himself up? Then is it always and necessarily cowardly pride and proud cowardice that doesn't want to

9. Translator's note: 1 Cor 4:7.
10. Translator's note: Latin, "by grace alone."

agree with God against man? Or is there an "I'm not moving" in both directions, and can it also be impudent arrogance, to say quickly and too readily: I have *done* the sin (so that one finally has peace and quiet from the one who always wants to be right)? Is it *not* the same to say, "I don't say that I am not a sinner," and "I confess that I am a sinner"? So it is indeed. For the first statement leaves the judgment up to God; in the second, man accomplishes it himself. The former, however, is possible even if the latter should not be possible for man always and in every case for the sake of man's honesty (who is "not conscious of any guilt even if still not thereby justified") and for the sake of the honor of God (who can have mercy *how* he wants: preserving or taking away, maintaining or ceasing). There are, of course, cases—oh, there must be innumerable times—when man (no matter that he leaves the final judgment to God who alone searches hearts and reserves judgment to himself) must simply and honestly say: "I have sinned"; when this sentence, "in all probability" in the realm of human endeavor and its consequences before the world and the Church, alone sincerely expresses the facts, the truth of man in this expression of one's own conscience that has been found guilty by God's truth. And then it has to be said before God and the Church, inexorably and forthrightly. Then this sentence is the only forthright formula of the *confessio* of man that praises grace. But when this formula is not possible (and it is, as stated, not certain a priori, and may not be asserted as certain a priori that it is possible as a later determination of a new act of sin for every human being who was once justified), then isn't the denial of such a formula, for the sake of the integrity of man and the honor of God, an assertion that one is *not* a sinner? No. If I am not conscious of any sin, am I justified before God? (Cf. 1 Cor 4:4.) While thanking the grace of God (while trembling and hesitant), if I dare to say that I am not conscious of any guilt, then do I say presumptuously to God: "I am righteous before you"? Can't man soberly and objectively—while looking at himself—say: "I have fought the good fight, kept faith and love,"[11] and yet—while raising his eyes to God—sink down: "If you, Oh

---

11. Translator's note: Cf. 2 Tim 1:13 and 4:7.

Lord, kept a record of sins, Oh Lord, who could stand?"[12] Who
knows what is in man except God? Who can *ultimately* say (so
that he knows that his judgment can only be confirmed by God)
whether his selflessness is only a clever form of his egotism or
genuine, whether his kindness is the weakness of the cowardly or
the selflessness of the strong, whether his purity is basically pure
love or the inhibition of the weak, whether his faith is the great
trust in the true God or the cowardice that seeks the security of
the "for all cases" or wants to enjoy a religious-lyrical mood,
whether his uprightness is the love of justice or civil dressage?
Whoever senses the dark powers in the depths of his being, whoever experiences in his daily sins (here they receive a completely
different aspect and a heavier weight than before) that *everything*
is in him and everything is possible in him (is possible *through*
him), who can then still dare to say with final certainty that his
"I" (that acts, decides, and bears its final responsibility before
God) sits right there in this indistinguishable darkness of contradictory powers, has identified itself precisely with that which tes-
tifies and fights for God against the darkness? Who wants to say
(with final certainty) before God, not on the earthly marketplace
of life, whether the good in him is the fig leaf of his shame, of his
evil in him, or whether the evil is the not yet completely destroyed enemy of the decisively victorious good? Who wants to
say unequivocally that the "actual" in his poor rubbled-over
heart is he himself: the yearning for the stronger love of God or
the unacknowledged, bitter ill-will toward the ungauged demands of this love? Oh, we could only talk unequivocally if we
were so unequivocal that we could grasp the true unequivocality
of our person that does exist and that God sees. But fundamentally we cannot do this. Who knows that the most sublime kindness can be the precondition of a wickedness that perverts it with
the speed of lightning, that paradise is the place of the deepest
fall, that one can reject God's messenger in order to do a service
to God, that can hear the witness of his Son as a blasphemy—will
this one say before God: "I am justified before you"? Particularly
if his daily sins always convict him of how equivocal man is, and
he knows that even little things are seated very deeply, and that

12. Translator's note: Ps 130:3.

the most radical evil doesn't always have to demonstrate its presence with much aplomb? Or will man say (even when he is not conscious of any guilt): "I am a sinner"? How else is he supposed to sum up succinctly and simply *his* truth about *himself* than in this way, how else is he to say what he (without God's grace that always remains *God's* grace) himself is? He is always the one held by God, the one saved by God, the one lost by himself, the one impenetrable to himself, the one who can only be judged by God. How else could he confess himself to be this one than through the word "sinner"? Lord, you know everything, me, the sinner—and also the love which you work in me.

But (we are unfortunately not quite finished) if, what man *is*, already is, is seen before God (in all the misery of the yet unfulfilled and in every future possibility of a new decision) in its last detail (before God and his knowledge) but is unequivocal (be that as it may that *we* don't know it), how can we not know this, if this unequivocality is *our act*, our free, responsible act, an act for which we are only responsible insofar as we know about it, its quality before God? Don't we flee in order to save the indeterminableness of our condition, or our state of salvation, into darkness in which a free act is not at all possible as a responsible one, although the condition should unequivocally depend on the act, should even be identical with it?

In order to answer this question, we must know which "certain knowledge about ourselves" we have excluded, which "not-knowing," whether we are worthy of love or wrath, we have asserted. We have excluded the knowledge of reflection, of subsequent examination, of re-examined balance as certain, unequivocal knowledge. Not more. This, however, radically and fundamentally. That is odd and sounds improbable, but it is also necessary that one takes things as they are and may not make them more simple than they are on account of a "clear" (that is, meager) theory. In the spiritual life there is also something similar to the uncertainty principle. One wants to examine and precisely determine his act so that one knows "for certain" what one has from it, what one *has* done (previously). Thus one observes the act (in a subsequent reflection, no matter how quickly) and changes the act itself again because the observation itself is no neutral process of pure, objectively duplicating knowledge;

rather, is itself decision, act, moral or immoral sentiment, and as such lends a new characteristic, a new stamp, to everything earlier in man (therefore also the prior act that is to be observed) and thereby itself must occur as "unexamined." One cannot find a completely neutral standpoint outside of the item to be examined for such an audit of one's acts, for such an accounting of oneself (as possible, necessary, and useful as this is). The examination itself is an act, and its result (whether it is honest or perverts again the sentiment to be checked) can never be determined for certain without there being a *processus in infinitum*.[13] However, an examination is itself an item on the balance-sheet of "how one stands," and the darkest one if it wants to elucidate everything and bring it into order. If, however, man really wanted to say what his condition is, if he unequivocally (not only with the "moral" certainty of the everyday) wanted to know what he is like, then he would need this adequate possibility of reflection, which doesn't exist because man is always only "with himself" when he runs away from himself to the thing outside of himself (even what can be determined by reflection on his action is still "thing"), in which "he himself" is not mirrored unequivocally. And, therefore, there is no "objective," no expressible knowledge of an unequivocal nature, no "evidence" of principles about the individual himself. And in this sense, human action occurs really in the dark, and no one knows with unequivocal certainty (of just this nature), as the Council of Trent stresses, whether he is in the state of grace. And nonetheless there is a "knowledge" (or whatever one wants to call that judging light that accompanies it and is inseparable from the act) in which one knows what one does (not: has done) that accompanies the act so that it, in its innermost quality before God, becomes unequivocally responsible before him, so that one can never say: "I actually didn't mean it that way," and which knowledge dies out in the same moment (or only shines indistinctly) when man wanted to use it in order to judge himself with final unequivocality. One can also say: "If you don't ask me (indeed, if I don't ask myself), I know it; don't ask, otherwise I won't know it anymore." If the

13. Translator's note: Latin, "infinite progression," similar to "vicious circle."

judgment of God will bring the acts of our heart, of the hidden abyss, into the light, the man of reflection, of statements about himself (also *before* himself) will be surprised, but his heart will say: "Actually I have always known, known very well that this knowledge could be clarified." This unequivocally inexplicable knowledge of the innermost center of the *acting* (and only so!), knowing one will only be distinguished before God. It is not translatable into what we normally call knowledge of ourselves so that man can only judge himself by his acts. But this knowledge is there for this reason. One can call it what one will: ineffable basic fact, inexpressible self-knowledge of the *anima*[14] (in distinction to the comprehensible knowledge of the *animus*),[15] conscience (in the original sense of the word in that it lies "behind" reflection and reflectiveness), synteresis, *scintilla animae*,[16] or whatever. It exists, and it lies where freedom, knowledge about oneself, and I are still together inseparably in one root as much as this basis must go out into its "powers" in order to be what it is. Because this "light" and that "dark" exist, we always know who we are but cannot say it to ourselves and thus cannot confess it with that word that we also need when we confess to God what we know about ourselves. Because that is the case, man can (except for that witness with which the Spirit intercedes for the saints with *inexpressible* groans)[17] only say again and again to his God from the essential darkness of his situation: I am a sinner, have mercy on me. He would cease being a man of this earth if, in bitter impatience, he never wanted to actually know, never expressly to know "black on white" what he actually is like, to turn around, as it were, in order to watch the act of his life, in order to be the judge during his "race," whether he is on the right track and fast enough. He can only run, and because of all the running—away from himself to God—forget thinking about the fact that he is running. And because only the runner is justified before God, and we are all still running and must forget what is behind us (even if the decisive thing had already been attained),

---

14. Translator's note: Latin, "soul."
15. Translator's note: Latin, "intellect," "reason."
16. Translator's note: Latin, "the spark of life."
17. Translator's note: Cf. Rom 8:26-27.

therefore, the actual prayer that we have to say to God about *us* is never, "I am in your grace," but always, "have mercy on me a sinner." *Humiliter et veraciter,* we can all say this because all justice is his grace alone, and because we never know whether we have it but do know that we shall never have it by ourselves. Surely finite man never expresses everything that he is supposed to say in one prayer. Therefore the prayer of guilt is never the only prayer, and the fifth petition is never the entire Our Father. The prayer of guilt, the joy of the love of God, the thankful praise of grace, the blessed word of unshakable hope, the sober petition for bread, the self-forgetting prayer for others, the extolling praise of his great splendor—only all of this together is the prayer of the Christian. There is no formula for this unison of the choir. As the Spirit inspires us, is how we want to pray.

8

Prayers of Decision

The moments and times in a human being's life are not equal. The external time of the physicist and the watchmaker flows along evenly. Each moment is equally long and also equally important, since exactly as much can happen in each of them. But it is different in man's inner life. There are moments that are seemingly empty, others that are unspeakably full. Moments in which nothing occurs, in which nothing can occur even with man's best will, and others in which, in a certain sense, all of man is present with his earlier life and with all his powers. Moments which are filled with the entire concentrated power of the inner man in which, therefore, events happen; facts are created which endure, which cannot be undone and thus determine the life that follows forever or for a long time. In such moments, man is totally within this together with his entire past, from whose experience he acts, and also with his future, which he determines and thus already anticipates. These are moments which can determine a life and an eternity. Moments of decision.

The choice of a profession can be this type of moment, or the assent of loyalty and love that binds one's life to another human being for ever, to his life and destiny; or a vow made to God, or other acts which have substantial, perhaps in many respects irrevocable consequences even in civil life.

But such decisive moments are not necessarily outwardly noticeable or even connected with some sort of external ceremonies. Such moments can come in eerie silence, quite quietly and as matter-of-fact, without announcement, quite unexpectedly. Man's way of life over its boring, well-known terrain suddenly takes a turn. Suddenly a life-or-death situation arises in man's interior—even if outwardly everything remains as before, very innocent and everyday. For example, whether one grasps the decisive chance in one's development of character or misses it, the chance once missed will not return for a long time or even never. Perhaps one is suddenly asked by life, no, by God, whether one wants to stand up for truth or for a lie; whether for a just cause or for unjust private profit; whether he wants to ennoble the spiritual man in himself through faithfulness in his love or wants to degenerate to bestial carnality through unfaithfulness. And also in these matters of inner, moral man, there are not always such hours of decision. When they do occur, they are often of a no longer humanly revocable effect. Also in this area, there are actions which hardly touch the core of man, and others which are decisive for the character of the entire inner man. And these are the actual moments of decision.

In such moments of decision, however, man stands in his life seemingly "eye to eye" with God. He senses—in that incomparable feeling that only befalls man during an encounter with God and that therefore has no name—that he is touched by God. For ultimately this situation of decision is one which, correctly viewed, man can never give to himself; rather, it comes over him and is brought about by God himself. This decision is basically always a decisive answer to a question that *God* directs to us. This decision is an answer to the question of the soliciting love of God, to the question of the unconditional faithfulness to his will. For this reason, this decision always goes basically over our relationship to God. Therefore moments of decision are always moments of God when God's eye looks at us, and our look meets his. They are moments from which an eternity will live. But during such moments of decision, when the eyes of God and man meet, then such moments are moments of prayer, presupposing only that during them man gives the correct answer, the answer of love. For during them God asks with the divinely quiet vehemence of his infinite love, which is unspeakably persistent and inexpressibly discreet. When, however, man says yes to this question, what else could one call this than prayer? Therefore there are prayers of decision because just decisions are always prayer. For they happen before God and around him. We want to consider three such prayers of decision somewhat more precisely: prayer during temptation, prayer in the decision of contemporary time, prayer for the decision of death.

The life of man on earth is trial and temptation. That is the situation of life for which no complaint or regret can help, which simply must be seen and accepted and endured. And this temptation to sin is—even if not the same always and everywhere and for everyone—*genuine* temptation. It attacks man unexpectedly, it has in man *himself* an ally, his hunger for good fortune, his sadness and the melancholy of life that lusts for an anesthetic, his trust in the concrete, his mistrust of the future hereafter, his amazing and uncanny facility for moral counterfeiting which can make good evil and evil good. And not only for others and before others but also for himself. A falsification that occurs in the first part of our moral judgment, in those preconditions of our moral judgments that we presume as self-explanatory and are not at all in question, a forgery that not only falsely measures but changes the standards themselves until sin and the perverse have been conjured into virtue and uprightness.

The temptation is genuine temptation. That also means that it strikes us, when it really (which is not the case every day) comes as great and decisive, when we are too weak. That is not to say that we necessarily must succumb to it. Oh no! But that is supposed to say: The great and decisive temptations strike man and conquer him if he doesn't become stronger than they are. Man is not—the opposite would be a deceitful illusion—always in lasting, fully ready, immediately available possession of all of his moral powers, all those powers which he needs to overcome decisively and finally the heavy burden of a real temptation. Almost unavoidably man has times of exhaustion, times of coolness, perhaps of a certain irritability, times in which for him God, eternal life, the radiant light of moral virtue, of truthfulness, of purity, of justice, of faithfulness, and so forth, appears as distant and dim and as a luxury which one can only afford in good times. He has times on the other hand in which desire, success, wealth, comfort, stand before him manifestly and have already filled his blood and soul with their sweet enticement, have seemingly already burdened him with the craving that is blind to the spiritual law of higher man, who is God's, have burdened him before

he was ever asked how he plans to take a position on this retun-
ing of his inner man. It is as if genuine temptation, before it officially attacks, already had been secretly in the fortress of the
soul (as with a fifth column) and had very substantially lessened
the resistance forces. The genuine and dangerous temptation
strikes man in such a condition. Thus he will only be victorious
if he gains new forces *during* the battle. If he wants to endure
the battle with the resources with which he began, he will lose in
the long run. If he wants to conquer with the moral disposition
in which temptation attacks him, he will perish. If he wants to
fight in the narrow corner of comfort, of self-sufficiency, of in-
dolence, in which he had to begin the battle, he will not be victorious. Man must grow during temptation, the breadth of
eternity must be his chosen battlefield that must be dictated to
temptation. The stars of heaven must light his way, the violent
wind of the Spirit must pervade his soul. He must have the taste
of eternity on his tongue, the passionate love for God must fill
his heart anew as in wild passion and jealousy, the tablets of the
divine values must arise anew before his spirit in their sublime
majesty. Something must arise in him which is indistinguishable
from grace and freedom, which is a contemptuous, hard laughing about man, who we also are, the man of selfishness, of pleasure, of weakness, and of cowardice. A free and courageous fury
must arise above ourselves, above the cowardly deceit that always
wants to falsify our standards when they become uncomfortable
for us. A proud fury must arise over our heart which desires consolation over faithfulness, happiness over trial, and itself over
God. Then, only then is man the true soldier of God, a fighter
who deserves a victory, if he is armed against temptation; indeed,
then temptation is already conquered.

But how does the man of convention and everyday half-
measures transform himself during temptation, the man in whose
blood the lure of sin already is circulating, who—as in a stupor—
no longer correctly knows where he actually is: in a brutal, arrogant drive *or* in his oh so weak and intimidated conscience, how
does this man of the earth transform himself into the man of
God, into the man into whose hand the angel suddenly places
the flaming sword and covers him with the clarity and sweetness
of God as with a garment? Oh, this change doesn't happen when

we, tired and sluggish, begin a dispute with temptation with the hidden intention of letting ourselves be conquered. It doesn't happen when we are only negotiating so that we don't have to admit our capitulation at the defeat. This change does not happen when we may not want to fall but also not grow, when we may not want to be conquered but also want to be housed as close as possible to the enemy. This change only happens when we pray. That means when the temptation of desire, the temptation of weakness, of cowardice, of hate, of vengeance, of unbelief, of blind obstinacy, of bitterness, and the like rises within us and in our flesh, then the ultimate and the inmost must rise up that can only be taken in by temptation when "we" ourselves open up to it (but we would do it constantly if this center of man could not succeed in making the *entire* man again subject to the law); let this inmost of man rise up! It should begin to shout wildly and with determination as one who fears for his life, to scream to God angrily and hard against one's own flesh and tempted spirit. Let this inner man flee to God, don't let him stay by himself, let him flee from his weakness to the power of God, from danger of his own unfaithfulness and of his own treason to the eternal faithfulness of God. He should beg for love, he should scream for the Holy Spirit, he should shout for the power of the cross of Christ from whose grace alone man finds the courage, in the death of denial of the hunger for life, to choose the life of righteousness, of truth, and of God! During temptation man should not speak with temptation but with God; with God not about temptation but with God about God, about his grace, his love, and his life. If the serpent accosts man, let it find no one who listens and speaks with it. Let its first word, "Why?" be a challenge not to ask the serpent about the reason for the law but to talk with God, the single and eternal Reason, to worship this final Reason of all reasons, to direct to him all our heart's longing. Only the one who prays survives temptation because only through prayer does man become again that one who in the holy incomprehension of God's child does not comprehend the enticement of sin and despises it. Genuine temptation always finds us weaker than we should be, for otherwise our appetite and the inclination wouldn't reply to it from within. The conquest of temptation can only happen through the conquest of such appetite and inclination. But that only happens through man's new desire and inclination in his heart for God. That, however, is prayer.

Therefore pray during temptation! Learn to pray! During temptation don't say to yourself, "I can't," say to God, "You can." Don't tell yourself, "I can't exist and live without 'that'" (which you should forgo); say to God (say it loudly and always, say it patiently and stubbornly): "I can't exist without you!" Don't say to renunciation, "You are the death of my inward man," say to it, "You are the rising of true life that only begins living by dying!" Shout for clarity that isn't deceived when temptation is disguised as an angel of light, when the man in you is the lie that knows a thousand reasons why the everyday sober law of God doesn't apply in your case when he gives you a subtle and even pious lecture about why your situation is unique and can't be measured with normal standards! Pray that you may remain immune from the mystique of sin that Paul already condemned when he says (Rom 6:1): "Shall we persist in sin that grace may abound? Of course not!" God's grace can lift the *poor* sinner up from his fall. Woe to him who, having fallen, will not believe this, who will not let God be greater than his own guilt! But even more woe to him who, still standing, wants to fall to give God the opportunity to lift him up again! How does he know that God will lift him up? There are sins against the Holy Spirit that find forgiveness neither in this nor in the other life! Whoever wants to be redeemed through sin is not far from such sin. Today, however, the temptation to such sin is near to many. Pray for light during temptation!

We should acquire an inner flair which immediately becomes awake and notices whenever our inner power and joyousness, that inner sense of well-being, of spiritual health and vigor, decrease; which notices when bad moods, displeasure, annoyance, inner irritability at spiritual things, bitterness, appears in their place; whenever inner love and inclination to God dwindle and his burden appears heavy and oppressive instead of sweet and light. This flair should warn and admonish us to pray right away without anxiety and in joyous trust in God to regain through prayer that inner attitude again whose abatement we had just noticed. And that is valid more than ever when an actual temptation makes us notice that an actual condition of weakness of spiritual man exists in us. Then more than ever we are enjoined to seek God. Only when we come nearer to God shall we escape the enchanted circle of evil which otherwise will poison slowly—but with deadly certainty—our spirit, heart, and mind. Whoever does not want to succumb to temptation, but also doesn't want by praying to struggle above that inner lukewarmness of the heart—in which this temptation is only possible—will not remain victorious. For he has misunderstood the deepest nature of temptation. It is namely always an invitation of divine love. And the answer to this invitation is called prayer. At least prayer in some kind of form. Whoever is suffering from the compulsion of tenacious thoughts and impulses will often not do well, in the usual sense of the word, of *expressly* praying for release from the temptation. By such action he would entangle his inner awareness even more in the mesh of such thoughts and impulses. In such a situation the prayer meant here is the joyous reliance on God, the carefree peace with which man unperturbedly looks beyond the nightly specters of his interior into God's free world and to his work and heartily proceeds to the day's agenda. But even such tactics of the spiritual battle are indeed watching for God, are prayer.

Temptation is a moment of decision. And whoever prays during it will conquer it. For it is written: "Watch and pray that you may not enter into temptation" (Matt 26:41). Prayer during temptation is therefore a prayer during a decision.

We want to speak briefly about a second prayer of decision. About prayer in the *decision of contemporary time*. These years in which we now are living are a moment of decision more than many other times in the long history of humanity. Many things *have* already been decided. The scepter of the world has already passed from the West. The West, for which the promises of God were meant because it was supposed to bear the name of Christ before the kings and peoples of the entire world and *therefore* had become the ruler of the world. It has betrayed the mission of God in its entirety by the destruction of the unity of Christianity, by worshiping the golden calf, by the arrogance of faithless reason, by the self-seeking tyranny with which it wanted to seize the world for itself, and finally in the distortion of Christ's cross into the swastika. And therefore its sconce has been moved from the spot, and the mission of God and his honor in the world are about to be given to other peoples who will later more willingly bring in the fruits of the kingdom of God (even if they don't appear to us to be more worthy of the kingdom of God than we ourselves). Decisions have already been made. Decisions have been implemented in which the hard logic of history and the guidance of humanity, which has been filled with the hard inexorability of divine love toward the kingdom of God, are mysteriously at work. Developments that certainly contain a holy mandate that we may not hinder and shall no longer hinder. But in these developments and decisions that have already been made and have already begun, there are still immense possibilities, possibilities that will be fulfilled or eternally remain empty depending on how we ourselves will yet decide in these times, depending on whether we pray or not, possibilities in which God's irrevocable call to the West also is yet to become manifest, possibilities of further earthly curse or blessing, possibilities of real peace or new war, possibilities of vocation of the West to action and work in the history of the kingdom of God, possibilities for good and evil, for good fortune and misfortune which will also form our quite personal, quite everyday earthly lot happily or sadly. It is still an open question whether the West broke into pieces like the precious alabaster vessel of the Gospel so that its fragrance, the fragrance of its faith, its spirit, and its history more than ever fills the house of the whole world, or whether it broke into potsherds that are useless and are thrown away by the potter as a vessel of shame, poured out and empty. It is still open whether God grants these peoples of his thousand-year love a time of peace for stocktaking in their true vocation that simply consists of being Christian in the faith and that then everything else will be given into the bargain, or whether Europe slowly decays as the land of degenerate peoples who have become beggars in body and soul and spirit, or whether the West once more becomes the battlefield of the world that finally perishes in blood and tears before God lets his new times or the final day begin, or whether. . . . But who knows how to sense the possibilities of God which obey his word? Only one thing is certain: Even yet God can—in spite of all the "historical necessities" that for God, the Lord of history, are still a thousand times open—say to us what he once said to the ancient people of the covenant: "See, I set before you today life and prosperity, death and destruction. . . . This day I call heaven and earth as witnesses against you that I have set before you life and death, blessings and curses. Now choose life, so that you and your children may live and that you may love the Lord your God, listen to his voice, and hold fast to him. For the Lord is your life, and he will give you many years."[1] We still have many decisive things to choose. While standing amid the ruins of a thousand-year history, we can still lay claim to the right and have the courage to pray for the happy, the great, and the sublime for this people and this Western history. For just these times, the Lord himself called us to prayer through the mouth of his mother, which is supposed to be a power in the contemporary history of the West and the world. Will we pray? Will we as Christianity and as a people finally pray, pray often, pray innerly, pray for the kingdom of God and for a new pardon for the history of our nation, even as little as we can imagine how it is supposed to happen? Will we pray with the confidence of faith that hopes against all hope? Or will we remain hardened and callous in misfortune or indifferent and listless, human beings who only care to save the pitiful bundle of their own advantage from the common conflagration, let happen what may to the others and the nation? Or will each wait with such prayer until the other, until all, have begun because no one feels responsible for this prayer of common decision, because—as in the recent past—each recognizes his duty as his own when it is commonly recognized and thus has become harmless and effortless?

We are living in times of world-historic decisions which are yet to be made. Will they find us praying in such a manner that they can be the answer of God's mercy to this prayer?

A third prayer of decision is the prayer for the *decision of death*. Our death is the moment of decision pure and simple. For truly man's entire life is collected into this moment, into this moment everything about this life becomes unequivocally firm and final, in death our time and our life become eternity. This way or that. In death God and man both speak their last word, the word that stays and never again dies away but remains permanently in the ear and heart, now and always.

1. Translator's note: Deut 30:15, 19-20.

Shall we have the grace to make this moment into a prayer, into the high-priestly prayer of our life that sacrifices everything and offers up everything, everything that we are and were, that we did and suffered, lifts it into God's light and sinks into the abyss of his mercy? Shall we die knowingly and lovingly, will our dimming eye recognize *that one* in death who meets us for the last time in that form in this life, that one who himself has died and yet, behold, he lives, Jesus Christ? Shall we say to him in this moment, "Yes, come Lord Jesus"? Will this our prayer be accompanied by the prayer of the bride of Christ, by the Church's "prayer of faith" (Jas 5:15) when she anoints us as kings of eternity? Shall we be able to pray in this hour of decision and praying offer our spirit into God's hands? May our merciful God grant us the grace to leave this world praying so that the heart's last word in this time could be the first of eternity that never ends! Blessed the one who is able to speak such a prayer of decision *during* the decision itself!

But we don't know whether this grace will be granted to us, to approach death consciously and in the freedom of the spirit, and praying to greet it as the messenger of God. For death comes as a thief in the night. And we have no guarantee that our last word of decision about time and eternity won't fall in a moment when we are not thinking of death, that it is a word which we ourselves don't know that it was the end of our answer to God. Thus we can't do anything else than to keep the lamp of faith and of love burning now and always, than always to be supplied with the oil of good works, than always to watch so that when the Lord comes, he doesn't find us sleeping. We can do nothing better now than to pray often and always the prayer of decision that we want to speak *in* the hour of our death, to be a prayer now *for* the decision of that future hour, to pray now for the grace of perseverance. To pray now: "Let me never be separated from you; and when I want to leave you, oh, my God, then don't let me, you God of hearts, of the weak and bold, force my rebelling heart into your service with the omnipotence of your mysteriously gentle grace!" To think now of one's death is a good prayer. A prayer of decision. When the uncertainty of the hour of death forces us to anticipate the prayer of decision *during* death in an everyday prayer *for* the hour of death, then the prayer of everyday and the prayer of decision are entwined. And both mean that one must pray constantly and not desist.

We have spoken many words about prayer. Perhaps fewer words would have been better. But then we have said almost nothing about prayer and much that is important was completely passed over. For example, we should have spoken about one thing during this period because it is a substantial precondition of true prayer, which Isaiah alludes to when he says (58:7-9): "When you break your bread with the hungry and take the poor homeless into your house . . ., *then* you will call, and the Lord will answer; you will cry for help, and he will say: 'Here am I.'" In the final analysis, talking *about* prayer doesn't matter; rather, only the words that we ourselves say to God. And one must say these words oneself. Oh, they can be quiet, poor, and diffident. They can rise up to God's heaven like silver doves from a happy heart, or they can be the inaudible flowing of bitter tears. They can be great and sublime like thunder that crashes in the high mountains, or diffident like the shy confession of a first love. If they only come from the heart. If they only *might* come from the heart. And if only the Spirit of God prays them together also. Then God hears them. Then he will forget none of these words. Then he will keep the words in his heart because one cannot forget the words of love. And then he will listen to us patiently, even blissfully, an entire life long until we are through talking, until we have spoken out our entire life. And then he will say one single word of love, but he is this word itself. And then our heart will stop beating at this word. For eternity. Don't we want to pray?